YOU
TURN

ADVANCE PRAISE FOR THE BOOK

'In *You Turn*, A.V. Anoop invites readers on an incredible journey that highlights his adaptability and accountability, as well as his strength of enduring relationships. This work is more than just an autobiography; it's an engaging guide for those ready to embrace their journey and pursue their aspirations. His insights are deep, his honesty refreshing and his story is genuinely inspiring—a must-read for anyone looking to live a fulfilling life'—**Hon'ble K. Kailashnathan, IAS (retd), lieutenant governor of Puducherry**

'My good friend Anoop, who I have known for almost three decades, is a multifaceted and multitalented personality—an entrepreneur, philanthropist, theatre artist and film-maker to name just a few. Anoop has evolved over the years. He was very close to my late father Shri K.K. Rajendran (Chakyar Rajan). He looked up to him as a friend, philosopher and guide. My father told me that Anoop is a keen learner and has the ability to handle any situation life throws at him with rock-like endurance. *You Turn* walks you through Anoop's life and shows how perseverance and hard work are some of the keys to success. Anoop comes out as a social reformer and role model of good conduct. His work speaks for itself. This book is a good read. I wish Anoop all the best in life. *Lokah samastah sukhino bhavantu* [May everyone, in the whole world, be happy]'—**Hon'ble Justice K.R. Shriram, chief justice, Madras High Court**

'My good friend A.V. Anoop's autobiography, *You Turn*, makes a delightful read of how he made a mark in the many roles he has played in his life. Beautifully adapted to English from its original form in Malayalam . . . the journey of a man who is continually seeking to learn and evolve. A must-read for all who wish to be inspired'—**S. Somanath, chairman, Indian Space Research Organisation**

'Dr A.V. Anoop's book *You Turn* is not merely an autobiography but also a "do-it-yourself" book, which reveals the secret of his success as an industrialist, businessman, a medical specialist, film-maker, actor, social activist and now an author. He expects "you" to "turn" to a more productive path after reading this book. But it is hard to emulate his ways and methods, as they dictate a life of devotion, hard work, a sense of justice and altruism. Nevertheless, it is certain that he is a role model for young people who are interested in a successful pursuit of life. The insights in the book are deep, his honesty is transparent and his story is inspiring. It is heartening to see that the book is now available in English for a wider audience. The English translation is as elegant and purposeful as the original in Malayalam' —T.P. Sreenivasan, IFS (retd), former ambassador and author

'Every experience is an experiment in life. The lessons learnt from such experiences enrich one beyond management textbooks and entrepreneurial handbooks. Instances and testimonies sketched by A.V. Anoop in this book are truly inspirational for all who are chasing their dreams. *You Turn* certainly is a compelling read!'—Sibichen K. Mathew (IRS), bestselling author and senior civil servant

'Dr A.V. Anoop's *You Turn* highlights resilience and creativity in the face of adversity. His journey illustrates how determination and passion can help navigate life's challenges, showing that obstacles can lead to remarkable achievements'—Dr Geethakrishnan, research unit head, WHO Global Traditional Medicine Centre, Jamnagar

'Dr Anoop displays masterly vision in *You Turn* . . . a practical and inspirational handbook for those on the fast track of enterprise'—Mammen Mathew, *Malayala Manorama*

'A compelling narrative of an inspirational entrepreneurial and philanthropic journey. A brilliant epitome of embracing counter-conventional mindsets to seize opportunities and overcome challenges'— Issac John Pattaniparampil, managing editor, *Khaleej Times*

'One of India's leading entrepreneurs, a known film-maker, philanthropist and activist, A.V. Anoop shares the stimulating story of his survival and growth in this rare and honest autobiography. There is neither narcissism nor self-pity here, though there is plenty of scope for both in his real life, of suffering, struggle and success. An inspiring life story written in an invitingly lucid style'—K. Satchidanandan, poet, president, Kerala Sahitya Akademi and former secretary, Kendra Sahitya Akademi

'An impeccable and exhilarating vision of his life . . . The author narrating his perilous path of life, pursuing effortlessly in several verticals of business, engaging with unforeseen anomalies of life, fighting and learning the art of overthrowing obstacles, entertaining himself while crossing this treacherous journey of existence with his passionate interest in arts, music and film-making.

Transporting the readers to his world, overflowing with his fulfilled dreams and visions, tons of happiness and loads of achievements still pursuing for the unknown . . .'—**Ravi Kottarakara, president, Film Federation of India and South Indian Film Chamber of Commerce**

'A versatile personality, Mr Anoop's life is one of resilience, taking responsibility for one's path as much as destiny, nurtured on lasting relationships, leaving all of us with great respect for the person he is. A must-read for a rewarding life!'—**A.R. Unnikrishnan, managing director, Saint-Gobain India Pvt. Ltd**

YOU TURN

A Memoir

DRIVING THE LEGACY OF THE WORLD'S BESTSELLING AYURVEDIC SOAP, MEDIMIX

A.V. ANOOP

**PENGUIN
BUSINESS**

An imprint of Penguin Random House

PENGUIN BUSINESS

Penguin Business is an imprint of the Penguin Random House group of companies
whose addresses can be found at global.penguinrandomhouse.com

Published by Penguin Random House India Pvt. Ltd
4th Floor, Capital Tower 1, MG Road,
Gurugram 122 002, Haryana, India

Penguin
Random House
India

Originally published in Malayalam by DC Books 2023
First published in Penguin Business by Penguin Random House India 2024

Copyright © A.V. Anoop 2024
Translated from Malayalam into English by Geeta Nair

10 9 8 7 6 5 4 3 2

ISBN 9780143472995

Typeset in Sabon LT Std by MAP Systems, Bengaluru, India
Printed at Replika Press Pvt. Ltd, India

www.penguin.co.in

MIX
Paper | Supporting
responsible forestry
FSC™ C016779

Contents

Foreword   ix

Author's Note   xiii

1. The Windows That Open to My Philosophy of Life   1

2. A for Amma, A for Ambalanagar   5

3. Pranks   10

4. The First Performance and an Audition   22

5. On to the Never-Ending Path   31

6. Single Room to Corporate Office   42

7. The Birth of 'Sanjeevanam': My Thoughts
    on Healthy Living   57

8. Tradition of Preceptors and the Film
    Yugapurushan   67

9. A Time of Love and Floods   75

10. Centenary of the Malayalee Club and
    My Organizational Ventures   91

11. King Oedipus and the Limp   109

12. How I Define . . .   117

13. A.C. Govindan and Infinite Knowledge   121

14. Nayanar: A Politician with a Difference   126

15. Some Lessons for Success in Business   129

16. Kerala and Tamil Nadu: Woven Together 137
17. Spectacular Sights during Travels 141
18. Accursed Words and Some Unusual Occurrences 148
19. Death of Dr Sidhan and the Unspoken Words 150
20. Medimix @ 50 152
21. In Memory of an Intrusion 156
22. A Good Turn Turns Sour 159
23. A Jammu Kashmir Raid 164
24. The Birth of the AVA Group 167
25. The Future 170

Foreword

What first struck me about A.V. Anoop's charming memoir, *You Turn*, is just how forthright it is. Here's a trailblazer who, having surmounted formidable odds, straddles sundry fields from entrepreneurship to education, philanthropy to film-making with panache. Yet, over the course of this exquisitely written book, not once does he project himself as a clichéd underdog, a protagonist who eventually triumphed merely because he was once embattled. Indeed, even when Anoop delves into the most tragic vicissitudes of his life, chief among them his father's sudden and untimely passing (which thrust upon his young shoulders the onerous burdens of heading a family), he doesn't want us to feel sorry for him; he wants us to see how, with fortitude and grace, we too can overcome the woes that beset us. It's no wonder, then, that his memoir, doused in impeccably wry humour, is a delight to read. And I'm certain you'll race through it, much like I did!

In *You Turn*, we have an endearing and resolute hero who never, even when he could, chose the easier way out, striving always to attain lofty heights by the dint of his hard work and razor-sharp mind. Finding himself mired in a morass of red tapism, Anoop, rightly disgusted by this deplorable reality of Indian life, spurned the governmental job that his father's passing away had entitled him to. As mavericks do, he drew the tides of destiny into his hands and dove into uncharted waters. Thus was born an iconic entrepreneur whose only training in business management were the missives that his maternal uncle sent him every day by train, from Madurai to Chennai. If this isn't the stuff of legend, I don't know what is. In the event, Anoop acquired the tricks of the trade on the fly. It was doubtless a laborious process, which in the early days of Medimix involved grappling with irksome litigation and toiling around shops near railway stations in Maharashtra to purvey soaps, even if just two or three could be sold at a time. Above all, Anoop's is a story of perseverance, of not giving up at any cost, come what may. For if you soldier on through the bleak night, a scintillating dawn is sure to greet you sooner or later: to this *You Turn* bears witness. As I neared the end of the book, I couldn't help turning over in my mind the last line of Tennyson's 'Ulysses': 'To strive, to seek, to find and not to yield.'

This, I believe, captures the essence of Anoop's life. Immersed as they are in the clamorous din of their ventures, it's rare to find entrepreneurs who manage to keep aflame their artistic spirit. But, of course, Anoop is a singular exception to this norm. Having been a thespian, one who gloried in being on the stage since his collegiate days, Anoop never, despite the exigencies of life, abandoned his passion for acting. In fact, he also transitioned over time into a masterful film-maker, with his movies and documentaries winning both state and national accolades. But the two laurels he considers the jewels in his crown are being feted in the Kilimanoor Palace, precisely where Raja Ravi Varma painted those masterpieces, for his documentary *Before the Brush Dropped*, and being honoured by the Indian Space and Research Organisation at their Bengaluru headquarters.

These achievements would have been enviable even had Anoop been solely a film-maker; that he is simultaneously a leading entrepreneur, educationist, philanthropist and social worker is what makes him truly extraordinary. At the launch of *You Turn*, his stellar memoir, I wish him the best of luck!

Shashi Tharoor,
Member of Parliament for Thiruvananthapuram

Author's Note

The Strength of My Writing and a Word of Thanks

My revered grandfather, A.C. Govindan, was a well-known writer. My father, A.G. Vasavan, used to write humorous articles in various publications. They have played an important role in developing the love for books in me.

I have gained remarkable recognition in different fields but did not have the courage to try my hand at writing. But the change in attitude brought about by the special way of life during the time of the Covid pandemic led me to start writing.

I wanted my words to come from the heart and be true to my experiences. I was determined to avoid exaggeration and boasting about my life story. Many things that seemed important had to be left out. Still, I am grateful for what I have been able to do.

Many people have supported and encouraged me in this endeavour. I am especially thankful to Sri Shashi Tharoor, the famous writer and a Member of Parliament, for having written his opinion about this book. I remember with gratitude my friend and a writer of repute, Sri Sajeed Khan Panavelil, who read the manuscript and helped in dividing it into chapters according to the subject matter.

I would like to extend my heartfelt thanks to Ms Geeta Nair for her exceptional translation work, as well as to my wife, Priya Anoop, and my daughters, Lanchana Vivek and Pratheeksha Prasanth, for their unwavering support and encouragement in helping bring this book to life.

1

The Windows That Open to
My Philosophy of Life

The Beginning

The first song of *Gitanjali*, the Nobel Prize-winning composition by our world-famous poet Rabindranath Tagore, goes:

Thou hast made me endless, such is thy pleasure.
This frail vessel thou emptiest again and again,
and fillest it ever with fresh life.
This little flute of a reed thou hast carried over hills
and dales, and hast breathed through it melodies
eternally new. At the immortal touch of thy hands
my little heart loses its limits
in joy and gives birth to utterance ineffable.
Thy infinite gifts come to me only on these
very small hands of mine. Ages pass, and still thou
pourest, and still there is room to fill.

Like Tagore, I too owe my thanks to whatever power governs the world for the life I have been given. That power has made me a businessman, an actor—on the stage and the silver screen—a film producer and one who offers service for the welfare of my fellow beings through the many organizations I am associated with. The power has also left in me the enthusiasm to do much more. But do not think that one can leave everything to that superior power and wait for results. Hard work is the only mantra that succeeds in business, as in any other field.

From the carefree life of a college student and the son of a high-ranking government officer, I was thrown into the sea of life quite unexpectedly. Once at sea, I learned to survive and started my first business enterprise by driving a taxi van. Later, I hired a driver so that I could better focus on my business.

The first real step I took was when I decided to waive my chance of being a government servant and opted to enter the business world, as suggested by my uncle, Dr Sidhan. My uncle used to make an Ayurvedic soap, Medimix, in his Chennai kitchen, with only his wife to help him. When he wanted to expand his business, he established a small factory and employed a few men from Kerala to work in it. But labour trouble forced him to stop production. It was at this time that he asked me to join the company. With the support of the entire family, we took the company from its humble beginning to a level where, today, we are at par with international brands.

If I can say this today, it is only because I was ready to see a crisis as a challenge and sought ways to surmount it.

I have witnessed the fall of many companies that had come up with a lot of fanfare. What led to their untimely exits are the lack of proper planning and money for capital investment. There is also the false belief that doing business is an easy job—a belief that they gather on seeing the success of only a few. Most of those who venture into the world of business are unaware that it requires a lot of thought, supported by an ardent desire to succeed. Strategies that are ethical and firmly rooted in the welfare of the society are essential for the success of any enterprise. Many carry the false impression that if there is enough money, anyone can start a business. Money is definitely important, but it is only one among the innumerable factors needed for success.

Medimix started as a small venture in the kitchen and rose to its present position of a leading Ayurvedic brand, with over 25,000 tonnes of soap manufactured annually. An atmosphere of trust exists at all levels in our company and anyone can approach me if they have any queries. We do not expect the children of our employees to work for us; rather, we help them get educated and seek varied options.

Medimix is today the largest selling Ayurvedic soap in the world. It is one of the 100 most trusted brands in India and used in about 10,000 hotels and resorts across the country. Brands have to depend on adverts and a ton of marketing, but Medimix has never resorted to celebrity advertisement. For us, Medimix is the star. Today, some well-known celebrities on the silver screen have featured in advertisements for Medimix.

My association with various organizations such as the World Malayalee Council, which is engaged in promoting the welfare and empowerment of Malayalees living across the globe, keeps me updated on latest ideas and strategies. Moreover, my indulgence in dramatics, not even remotely connected with the world of business, keeps my mind and heart fresh and healthy. From the time I lived as a small boy in a colony at Thiruvananthapuram, I have involved myself in organizing various events and meetings. This organizational capacity will always help in whatever profession you choose to follow. The latest in the line of positions I have been entrusted with is as chairman of the India Eurasian Trade Council. I have been a sportsman till an injury halted my ambitions, but the sportsman spirit

I gathered in the early days from the playing field has helped me deal with different types of people and life situations. Reading has been an unyielding passion. The new world you witness through the pages of literature holds more than what can be gathered from the umpteen textbooks on management.

Through this collection of incidents and lessons I've gathered from my life, I hope I can help and inspire others in different fields. There are no special skills exclusively reserved for a businessman. All life skills are important.

As a teenager who failed to clear his first audition, I have gone on to act in many films, even with legendary stars like Rajinikanth.

From selling our soaps on a bicycle to selling them in the international market, we have indeed come a long way.

Today, if I have to make a welcome speech or address a gathering, I can do so with confidence and conviction.

All this has happened because I was not ready to retreat in the face of challenges. Self-confidence has to be gained; it is not something you are born with.

To those who are ready to enter the world of business, love the work you are doing, love the product you are making and be a friend to your colleagues. Most importantly, have something more to look forward to in life. Making the most of your leisure time by spending it in enjoyable company will energize you for the hard day tomorrow.

There are no rules exclusively for success in business; all life skills that lead one to success are the ones needed for success in business too. I have titled this book *You Turn* as I felt that you have to learn from your own experiences and take new turns in life. It is your life; you must make the utmost effort to fashion it the way you want it to be.

2

A for Amma, A for Ambalanagar

'There is only one corner of the universe you can be
certain of improving, and that is your own self.'
—Aldous Huxley

Amma, Mother—the sweetest word I have ever uttered.

A word that comes from the bottom of the heart, loaded
with sincerity. It has a power of its own. It represents refuge
and relief. All life depends on it.

Life, in essence, is the sharing of the power of existence
with another. Life comes to a standstill once this sharing
is denied.

Life has been kind to me in many ways. The famous
axiom, 'When one door closes, nine others will open up
for you' has proved true for me. Life has taught me some
tough lessons. In essence, you should not panic when faced
with problems, as the equations to undo the difficulty are
contained in the problem itself. What you need to cultivate
is the expertise to discover that.

The words I scribe here are based on the lessons I've
learned. I am leaving the book of my life open before the
readers to point out what is what. As I pen down my life,
there are some basic truths embedded in it. There is also the

5

social responsibility that prompts me to write these words. I am trying to portray my thoughts and emotions with the same intensity with which I faced them. But it is up to you to decide how far I have succeeded in doing that. Such an assessment cannot be made in a few days or months. Still, I strive to root my words in truth.

My journey essentially touches upon varied phases of my life.

My aim is to tell, to recall; not to teach. But let me put forth some thoughts connected to my efforts. I believe in the soul that powers my words. This is the story of my life sans any exaggeration and flights of imagination.

What truly changed me are some unexpected events that go beyond any rational explanation. Once I remove myself from me, some truths and answers still remain. These form the topics of my writing.

It is a life of six decades; a panorama of unexpected events.

Joys and sorrows are part and parcel of every life. To enjoy the thrill of joy, one needs to experience sorrow. We see many lives ruined by the incessant search for joy, happiness; lives that did nothing good for themselves or the world. They were an unnecessary burden on the earth.

Many are the great men among us who dedicated their lives for mankind; treading the path of moderation lying between extravagance and miserliness. They dedicated their time, wealth, position and goodness for the welfare of others. They are the power and light in our lives; it is from them that we learn and move forward. They remain forever as the beacon of hope and persuasion. I harbour within my innermost self a desire to be like them. I pray that each word, each step, may lead me towards that goal.

There is no thrill in just being alive.

I am not born for that.

The thought that one should never hesitate to move on despite a feeling of helplessness; that each one of us has been sent to this world with a specific task to be fulfilled—these remain the foremost thoughts in my mind at all times. Some duties go beyond the scale of mundane materialistic achievements.

What we desire and what can be achieved may not always go hand in hand.

There was a time when I felt the world revolved around me—a graduate of the prestigious Mahatma Gandhi College at Thiruvananthapuram. That was also the time when my father left us forever. I will come to that in detail later.

Let me start from the beginning.

I started from *A*.

The first letter of the Malayalam alphabet. Also, the most important.

The first syllable in the Pranava Mantra, which is considered to be auspicious and the beginning of everything new. '*Aksharaanaamakaarosmi*,' says the Bhagavad Gita. ('Among letters, I am the letter A'.)

There is a couplet in the *Hari Nama Keerthanam* that declares the importance of the letter *A*.

The letter denotes Lord Brahma. The word *aksharam* (letter) refers to that which does not perish. In the realm of grammar, it is the first letter of the Malayalam alphabet; the first among the fifty-two letters in Malayalam. We constantly use fifty-four letters (*varnas*) and fifty-two characters (*lipis*). I was just recollecting what Kerala Panini A.R. Rajaraja Varma Thampuran, who compiled a treatise on Malayalam grammar and rhetoric, had said: 'There is no need to worry about my straying from my life to Malayalam grammar.'

But there is a grammar for life. For a faultless life, it is essential.

I was born on 30 April 1962 at 12 p.m. to A.G. Vasavan and Lilly Bai. My father passed away at the age of fifty-three. This happened when he was working in a high-ranking post as the director of fisheries in the government at Thiruvananthapuram. My mother is eighty-six. Upon the demise of my father, the four of us—me, Amma, my elder sister Anila and my younger sister Anjali: (the four As) as I would call ourselves—felt helpless and trapped within the four walls of the house.

We were living in Ambalanagar Colony in Thiruvananthapuram. Our mother was always a place of refuge for us. She was the daughter of Dr Padmanabhan, who belonged to the famous Cholayil Vaaliparambu family. Her father, who was serving as a doctor under the Thiru-Kochi government, only lived up to the age of fifty-six. When my grandfather passed away, my mother was just fourteen years old.

The Boy from Ambalanagar

All memories of my boyhood days are centred on Ambalanagar, a colony of about forty-five houses. We bought our first house here.

It was the time between boyhood and youth—a time when thoughts take wings. It was a happy time of freedom and enjoyment, with many companions of the same age.

Most of our neighbours were illustrious and successful in their own fields. Among them were Konniyoor Narendranath, director of Akashavani; Krishnamoorthy, who later became the DGP; Vijayapalan, principal of Law College; and Sivakumar, chief engineer, Kerala State

Electricity Board. Their presence offered immense support and care to us.

Holidays saw us coming together as the colony residents held competitions and distributed prize to the winners. The best time was during Onam. Boys and girls came together and enjoyed themselves with no undue restrictions. My foundation as an organizer and as an artist was laid while living in this colony. At one of the Onam celebrations, I recited a poem I had composed.

I still cherish the memory of many of those who lived in that colony—my friends Jacob Kuriakose, Sreekumar, Mathew Varghese, who later became a lieutenant colonel, Col Nagesh Nair, whom I used to address as Aniyan Chettan, as well as the many others who were uncles and aunties for us and the little brothers and sisters of those days.

I have no memory of any of the youngsters causing trouble or ruckus.

A happy life of six years among all those lovely people ...
And the story continues ...

3

Pranks

'The discipline of desire is the
background of character.'
—John Locke

Childhood is the time for pranks. The world is vast, with no walls or fences. A life close to nature. Electricity first came to our house at Vadookara in Thrissur when I was two years old. That was a life without AC, phone or car. Truth be told, no one felt these were important things back then. Agrarian activities such as harvesting in our paddy fields, the process of separating the grain and the straw by stamping on the stalks laid out on mats dominated rural life. A time when the cows and the haystack in the compound spoke of prosperity. There were bulls for ploughing the fields. The innumerable wild flowering plants and the fruit-bearing trees—the mango, jackfruit and tamarind—covered the compound. The aroma of ripe mangoes and jackfruit that filled the nostrils as the children walked along the ridges of the fields was heavenly. They could catch the small fish from the rivulets that nature had created—carp as well as the smaller *pallathi* fish. The *mundu*, the rectangular cloth that is worn around the waist, or the handloom towel, served as an effective net. During the monsoon, the field and the ridge would merge into a vast body of water. In summer, the mangoes would attract the children up the huge trees and the raw fruits would mostly be eaten there itself with some salt. Most of the vegetables for the house would be available in the compound surrounding the house. The cow dung and the ash, which were available in plenty, were used as manure. The number of coconuts in the trees and the measure of paddy in each house were considered the real wealth of the family. The guava and cashew trees provided delicacies for the children. Us children would build a fire with the dry leaves and twigs in the compound to get the kernel of the cashew. Many a time, we would suffer burns when we accidentally stamped on them.

But not all memories of those days are sweet. Life, as is evident, is a mixture of joy and sorrow. I was admittedly naughty. The pranks that I played on others are countless and my mother Lilly Bai was always ready to bear the brunt. I can attest that the words of the famous Malayalam novelist P. Kesavadev in his novel *Odayil Ninnu*—'The maternal heart is the court that pardons every wrong'—are true. In my youth, I troubled my mother a great deal. She would take me to the toilet, which, in those days, was at a far corner of the compound. The vast compound would be enveloped in total darkness by evening. There was no one to hear if anyone cried for help. Poisonous reptiles were there in plenty. Amma had to accompany me to the bathroom almost every night.

I joined the first standard at Guruvijayam L.P. School, which was about half a kilometre from home. As my father was busy with his official duties, it was my mother who took me to school for admission. My sisters and I had the chance to study in different schools at different places as our father got routinely transferred. While this helped us learn about different places and their culture and lifestyle, the constant movement from one place to another affected our studies. Before we could get familiar with one school, it was time to leave for a new place. In my experience, leaving the teachers, friends and neighbours so often was difficult but not a very saddening experience as I had the chance to explore new places.

I was ten years old when we were leaving Thrissur and going to Kozhikode. Our next-door neighbour in Thrissur was Velu, whom I addressed as Achachan. He was a police officer who revered the soil. He would advise everyone to live off the soil and demonstrated the same in his life. He was strict in matters of agriculture and in bringing up his children. His son, Lohithakshan, or Lohi, as I fondly called him, was my friend. I found delight in throwing stones at the mango trees in their compound and in turn got punished by my mother and Velu Achachan. Many years later, I had the good fortune to buy that land. As I visit it in my luxury car today, old memories of the tree, Lohi and those playful scoldings warm my heart.

The day before we left for Kozhikode, Lohi had come to my house. He was sad and he hugged me, his eyes welling up with tears. Lohi, who was older than me, lamented that he would have no friends to play with now. He invited me over to his house for duck curry. He considered this a farewell for his dear friend.

That evening, our neighbours heard Velu Achachan crying loudly near the pond in their compound. It was heartbreaking to see Velu lamenting near Lohi's dead body. His son had died by suicide, unable to withstand whatever sorrow assailed him. Lohi was only seventeen at that time. That incident pains me to this day. That memory strengthens my belief that parents, family and teachers should be cognizant of their children's mental health and be equipped to prevent such situations.

In my life, I've had the misfortune of being blindly punished by those who did not pause to ask for the reasons behind my actions. One of the most prominent accusations raised against me was when I was in the first standard. One day, I was walking to my school, proudly carrying what my grandmother in Madras had given me—a new umbrella and a steel box containing my books. No one else in my class had a box like mine. Some boys were playing with marbles on the path. As they saw me coming, they started throwing the marbles at my new box. As the marbles hit my box like bullets, dents and marks appeared on its surface. My most treasured possession was being damaged. I could not stand it. I attacked them with all my strength. The teacher appeared on the scene at that moment. She broke a stick from the tamarind tree nearby and started beating me. More than the pain inflicted by the stick was the humiliation at being punished for no reason. I instantly reacted. I lifted the teacher's sari and bit her hard on the leg. It was an action taken in haste and immaturity. Shocked by the unexpected pain, the teacher started chasing me down the street. The chase ended at the wall of the school. As I nimbly went over it, the teacher stood helplessly on the road.

This story of biting my teacher's leg spread fast. It reached my school also. My mother was summoned. The head master questioned me. I felt like a doe in the lion's cage. The waves created by this incident have not subsided in my home even today. Though my actions were extreme, I felt extremely hurt to get a beating when the other children were at fault.

Today, I am happy to see that we have various laws
to protect the rights of children. Justice Thottathil
Radhakrishnan, judge of the Kerala High Court, has, in one
of his judgments, asserted that even a child in the mother's
womb has rights of its own. Schools are institutions that
should lead the human race down the right path. Progress
should be shaped there. Teachers should be the most
revered in any society. They have the responsibility to bring
a good name and quality to education. There should be
no lapses on their part. Kunchan Nambiar, the legendary
Malayalam poet, has rightly pointed out that if the teacher
misses one alphabet, the children will miss all fifty-one of
them. (Malayalam has fifty-one letters in its alphabet.)
Teachers must be responsible for the safety and well-being
of their students, upholding the high principles propagated
by Mahatma Gandhi and Dr Sarvepalli Radhakrishnan. It
is heartening to see painful punishments such as pinching,
hitting by cane stick, throwing chalk pieces or the duster
at students and making students stand on the bench in
classrooms are history. The educational sector is becoming
more aware and supportive of children's mental health.
This is a welcome change.

The pranks I pulled on people around me did not
end with that 'bite'. I remember how, while in the fourth
standard, I wanted to fly like Hanuman and attempted this
stunt from the staircase of our house. I flew past six steps and
landed on the floor. My right hand was fractured and I had
to get it plastered. I was influenced by some of the action
scenes I watched in films. Watching the famous Malayalam
cine star Prem Nazir in films based on the Puranas and
Vadakkan Pattu, a collection of Malayalam ballads from
the medieval period that extols the abilities and daring of
some of the heroes from Malabar, I, too, wanted to mount

the galloping horses and fight my enemies. That desire prompted me to use our pet calf as a horse for me to ride. Once, as I jumped up and sat on him, he started running wildly. He kicked me down. That was when my hand got fractured the second time. My antics continued doing the rounds in our locality for a very long time.

I studied at St Joseph's School at Kuriachira, in Thrissur, Kerala, where we reached in a hand-pulled rickshaw. I was made to sit between my sisters, but I could never sit still. I would try my best to jump around in that limited space, putting the puller in danger of losing his balance. When my sisters tried to control me, I would pull their hair and attempt to jump from the rickshaw. The poor rickshaw-wallah finally gave up and informed my parents that it was impossible to take me in his rikshaw.

There was also the news of me breaking a poor woman's tooth with a stone. As far as I was concerned, she wasn't entirely innocent as she would threaten me with punishment whenever I met her. There are several other stories such as the one of me trying to jump up a tree thinking that I had acquired superhuman powers.

In retrospect, I feel that the children today are in a different world all together. The village of Vadookkara is still there in all its purity. Much has been lost in the incessant flow of time. The fields where the paddy swayed in its golden glory are not there. The hand-drawn rickshaws have largely disappeared though they still exist in some cities. Whenever I see them, my thoughts go back to those memorable rides to school in Thrissur. Another unforgettable experience during my school days is the time I got chickenpox. For relief from the itching and burning, I was made to lie on a bed lined with neem leaves and was under constant care and observation.

When it came to school, my mother was more worried than us when we had to appear for an exam. She would insist on sitting with my younger sister and me (Anu, as my dear ones call me) and go through the lessons. While I studied in the Malayalam medium till Class X, my sister studied in the English medium.

I did my Class V and VI at Chungam U.P. School in Kozhikode. Here, the style of teaching was entirely different from anything we had experienced before. Though all of us spoke Malayalam, my Thrissur slang clashed with their 'Kozhikodan' dialect, leading to much confusion. Most of the students in that school were the children of fishermen. As their families depended on their daily catch, their life became difficult during seasons when fish was scarce. The children coming from these households were not very studious or disciplined. Taking my books away without my knowledge, troubling me for no specific reason, all of these incidents were common. The subtle changes in my behaviour and language upset my mother. But as I passed through each class, I acquired a certain kind of maturity, unknown to myself.

In Class VII, I was transferred to St Rita's School, Ponnurunny, in Ernakulam. My most valuable learning from that place was training under the National Cadet Corps (NCC),[*] which I later joined. Initially, I was not interested in becoming an NCC member, but the lure of the special food given after each training session, which my friends praised a great deal, convinced me to join. In the first session, the trainer gave us a vivid description of

---

[*] NCC is the voluntary youth organization under the armed forces, working to train the youth to ensure the progress and the bright future of our country.

what the training aimed to achieve. The training helped in adopting a healthy and disciplined life and in being prepared during emergencies. Some teachers underwent training to take charge of the units at the school. The NCC cadets also got priority in admissions for further studies and in recruitment for the armed forces. Moreover, when cadets visited other states for training, concession was allowed in the train fare.

I was not all that interested in being present for the sessions and being in the hot sun during the training. But gradually certain parts of it started attracting me. I learned how to wear the cap and the boots that were a part of the uniform. The fact that there were precedents, specifications and rules even for the littlest aspects of the uniform caught my attention. As a part of the discipline, the shine of the shoes, the way the shoe laces were tied, wearing the cap firmly to prevent it from falling off during the parade and cutting the hair in a particular way, all of this was under scrutiny. Doing all these within a specified time showed how efficient one was. All the commands were given in Hindi, the national language. The commands and terms that I memorized during that time have helped me in crucial moments in my life. Today, we have Student Police Cadet (SPC) in place of NCC in our schools. The Student Police Cadet (SPC) Project is a school-based initiative by the Kerala Police.

After completing my quarterly examinations in Class VI, we shifted to Thiruvananthapuram. Till then, we had only heard about our capital city, the museum, zoo and some other attractions. We thought of it as the city with the Secretariat, residences of ministers, the Padmanabhaswamy temple, the radio station, airport and double-decker buses. I was grateful to get admission in the prestigious St Joseph's School, situated in the heart of the city. This was made easy because of my father's position as the joint director of fisheries. This institution maintained a higher standard than all the other schools I had attended so far, which also reflected in the demeanour and maturity of my classmates.

I had been under the impression that those who studied in English medium and spoke English were special. This had naturally led to a feeling of inferiority. In fact, the first rank in the SSLC examination for most years was secured by the students of St Joseph's School, a prestigious achievement in those days. People looked at the photo of the first-rank holder on the first page of all the newspapers and read his/her life history with much wonder and amazement. The school also shared in that glory.

I felt an urge to be on the same level with my peers. I knew that my interest in art and literature would help me achieve this. That belief was proved true later on in life.

Father Kuncheriya was the headmaster of St Joseph's School. Being a priest, he was determined to lead us along the path of strict discipline. He managed the school without neglecting any of the conventions of the Catholic priesthood. He would always walk around with a cane in hand. In turn, the students respected him with a tinge of fear.

Before the teachers entered the class, students would be talking, the noises easily leaving the precincts of the classroom. For Father Kuncheriya, this destroyed the disciplined atmosphere of the school. We didn't have any clue when the headmaster approached us and some of us had to bear his caning.

Father Kuncheriya was the embodiment of discipline for us. His demise at that time caused us much distress. He had fallen down the steps as he was coming out of a theatre in the city and succumbed to injuries. Being a strict Catholic priest, he did not support cinemas. But he had

gone to watch *Chattakkari* (1974), a Malayalam film by
the famous director K.S. Sethumadhavan, for a special
reason. Lakshmi was the heroine in it, portraying the role
of Julie, an Anglo–Indian girl from a Christian family.
Father Kuncheriya wanted to watch the film set in such a
Christian domestic background.

His sudden death pained us a lot. All the dissent we
harboured in our immature minds against the disciplinarian
dissolved immediately. The efforts that he took to bring
prestige and fame to the school are remembered even today.
It was during his tenure as the headmaster that the highest
number of students of that school secured the best ranks in
the SSLC examination.

There was an NCC battalion in St Joseph's School
too. Sri Varghese, who taught us English, was in charge
of the unit. He persuaded me to join, knowing that
I had been a part of it before. In Class IX, I was one
of the two cadets selected to participate in the annual
training camp, where NCC cadets from schools across
Thiruvananthapuram participated. The camp was in a
school atop a hill at Malayinkeezhu, on the eastern suburbs
of Thiruvananthapuram. Nothing matches the training
we received at that camp. It was similar to the kind given
to military personnel. We (hundreds of us cadets) were
assigned to make a road from the bottom of the hill to the
school. It was an adventurous and dangerous task as one
wrong step would have us fall down the hill.

On the first day of the camp, we realized that there
were no toilets for our use. Each one had to make one
for himself. It was to be made by making a hole in the
hardened soil. I could not even think of using such a hole
because I had never used such toilets before. So my primary
concern was how to avoid using the toilet till the end of

the camp. But the chapatti and the curry made with Bengal gram turned out to be the villain for me as I ended up having dysentery! I thought of escaping from the camp on that score. But I did not succeed; rather the authorities, being strict disciplinarians who believed in the efficacy of severe punishments, did not allow me.

So I continued my task of making the road; bruises appeared on my hands and they became swollen. Being out in the hot sun tanned my skin. The night duty was worse than all this. I had to stand guard for the camp with a heavy rifle that was much taller than me.

We were given training in aiming and shooting at the target. Pulling the trigger is an operation to be executed with immense care. While training to do it as one is lying on the ground, if the hand shakes, a kick is inevitable. Such intense training and severe punishment are given as the operation is extremely risky. If anyone accidentally closed their eyes on guard duty, a slap was sure to wake him up. All this made us feel a sort of revulsion and dislike towards the armed forces. But those ten days have certainly enabled me to face the dark and difficult situations in life boldly.

As the resentment against soldiers and armed forces still lingered, I decided to recruit high-ranking retired personnel from the armed forces in my company. I harboured a secret desire to be strict with them as some of them had done with me when I was in school. But I never had any ill intentions to hurt them at any time. Upon appointment, I observed that they continued to exhibit the same sincerity and discipline in my company as they had done in their service previously. My attitude changed, thanks to their sincerity and capabilities.

Later, I got the strength and self-confidence to ride a cycle to go around selling my soap, courtesy the training I received at the NCC camp.

What I have penned above are the memories of my ten years as a school student that still remain fresh in my mind.

4

The First Performance
and an Audition

'Men willingly believe what they wish.'
—Julius Caesar

Pre-degree—the two-year course before joining the degree
course—provides an escape from the strict atmosphere of
school. Now it is called the eleventh and twelfth standards,
or +1 and +2. Till a few years ago, pre-degree was a part
of college education so the boys and girls of the school step
into the college right after passing their Class X exams,
or what is commonly known as matriculation exam.
Schoolteachers are replaced by lecturers and professors.
There were no canes and punishments here. But there used
to be frequent fights between students, and colleges would
close down indefinitely.

I was admitted in Chinmaya Mission College,
Thiruvananthapuram. It was done to ensure that I imbibed
some moral values as the college was under the direct
supervision of the spiritual leader Swami Chinmayananda.
The boys who joined pre-degree classes in those days were
fewer in number than the girls. I too experienced this in the
first few days. Back then, the friendship between boys and

girls had a certain fragrance of purity and innocence. Now, after almost four decades, I feel there is a change in our culture.

In the relaxed life after the hectic schedule of Class X, I filled my free time with varied activities. I feel I should explain here what I mean by 'hectic schedule'. A student had to pass twelve examinations in Class X. For the pre-degree, it is just five papers each year. But it's not easy to pass those five examinations.

Apart from preparing for those exams, I practised three different skills during the holidays in these two years. One was the art of juggling. It is an interesting game where one tossed a number of objects into the air with both hands and caught them without letting them fall, only to toss them again. The eye and hand coordination must be perfect if this is to be successfully executed. I used stones for this performance much to the amazement of my audience.

The second activity I enrolled in was roller skating. After practising on the terrace of my house to balance my body and move forward on the small equipment with wheels worn on the feet, I ventured on to the street. Unless the skater is well trained, it may lead to falls and grave injuries. The third skill was in setting Rubik's Cube™. I could solve it within seconds, much to the amazement of my friends and family. The solving of Rubik's Cube™, where different formulae are applied, remains unattainable to most even today. My grandson Yuvaan is an expert in this now.

Another pastime I indulged in was listening to the audios of the films and plays that were broadcast on radio. I was enchanted by that wonderful world of entertainment and sounds. I enacted the parts of many of the characters in the plays and enjoyed listening to my own recorded rendition. I tried acting the parts of men, women, old people and children. In an attempt to better my performance, I bought the books with the scripts and tried perfecting my dialogues. Among these books, many were written by Sri Jagathy N.K. Achari (father of the veteran Malayalam cine actor Jagathy Sreekumar). R.L. Baiju, my relative, would join me in this and offer encouragement. This is how I became passionate about drama. As a sequel to this, some female students organized a stage play in college. In preparation for the presentation, all the actors studied their dialogues by heart. But none of us thought about rehearsals before the performance. The day of the presentation dawned. The curtain rose and the actors came on stage. The audience, mainly students of the college, waited anxiously. But the actors, seized by stage fright, could not utter the parts they had studied by heart. Our friends in the audience had little patience. They started booing with all their might. The actors left the stage in great haste and disappeared. That taught me never to venture into something without practise and familiarization. But this experience did not deter me from continuing to be involved with theatre and the stage, even as a student.

My first successful appearance as a hero in a play was at the park in the Ambalanagar colony. The play was based on a story written for us by our friend M.K. Jacob's mother. We had enough rehearsals and the presentation was a success. I played the part of a Muslim man.

Once Konniyoor Narendranath, director, Akashavani, came to know of my interest in drama. He put a medal around my neck and encouraged me to perform on stage. It was this encouragement that made me feel sure that I had my own role to play on the stage.

Later, at my request, he invited me for an audition at Akashavani. What happened there was nothing short of hilarious. I was seventeen at that time. I was asked to recite the part of a man talking to his wife on the first night after marriage and taken to the darkened recording room. The context and the words to be spoken were explained. The girl who was acting the part of the wife was in another dark room. The green light, signalling the start of the recording, was on. I started shivering. I could not be the 'husband'. The instructor felt that the reason might be that the girl, the 'wife', was in another room. So, he decided to bring the girl into the room where I was recording. To be alone with a girl in a dark room and enact our first night! It was beyond me. I forgot that it was only the audition for a radio play. My body started shivering even more. Thus, my first audition ended in failure.

When I look back on that incident, I think of many occasions later in life, when my sound was recorded at various Akashavani stations, as interviews and speeches. But my 'first night' incident never fails to bring a smile to my face even today.

I feel that it is necessary to present an idea of the exalted position held by the radio in the Seventies. One had to take a licence to use the radio. People depended on the radio for entertainment and news. The bicycle also required a licence. It had not become so popular in those days. Unknown to my father, I learned to ride using our neighbour's cycle. Later, that cycle was given to me as a present and I became my neighboour's much sought-after friend. It was my readiness to let them borrow my cycle and my expertise in games such as carrom and chess that elevated me to that position.

I was tall and slim. Most of the youngsters then used to fashion their hair into what we called a 'bird's nest' above the forehead. But I did not have that; I sported sideburns fashioned like the broad chisel used by carpenters. My friend recently sent me a photograph taken forty years ago. Photographs can make us revisit old times and recreate history. Trousers that had wide bottoms were 'bell-bottom pants' and those with even wider bottoms were 'elephant bottom pants'. I could be seen wearing both in my photos.

In those days, our father used to take me and my sisters to the Thiruvananthapuram Public Library. During the summer holidays, we would be there in the morning, carrying packed lunch with us. The library had the largest collection of books in the state, including some very rare editions. We would happily read and realized that books were the windows that opened to the world. Great literature is made with the light of knowledge and experience. They are the treasures of mankind. I quote these lines in speeches and classes even today.

Unfortunately, we could not enjoy the great books that the grand library housed to the best potential; we had not acquired the intellectual capacity to understand them at that time. What we really enjoyed though were detective novels; we had a special place for them in our hearts. That interest led me into reading other books. The novels by Kottayam Pushpanath played an important role in inspiring me to read other books. By evening, our father would come to pick us up from the library.

We saw that there was a separate section for books written by A.C. Govindan, my paternal grandfather. This distinction showed how great his works were.

The more I read, the more I felt the urge to write. I made up many stories and jokes and sent them to various publications. I still treasure those that appeared in print. I wanted to delve deep into writing but was deterred by the prevailing circumstances. I hope to overcome the loss of a chance to write more in those days by writing this book.

As I was maturing into a young man, the country was declared to be under Emergency rule in 1975. The word was heard repeatedly over the radio, but its real significance remained unknown. It was a rule proclaimed by Prime Minister Indira Gandhi. While those who supported her said that it was essential for maintaining the discipline and unity of the nation, those who opposed her argued that it was a declaration of war against the rights of citizens. The Emergency was withdrawn in 1977, but the waves in its wake still remain. That shows how closely people observe any rule that is imposed on our society.

I did my BCom from Mahatma Gandhi (M.G.) College, Thiruvananthapuram. My father wanted me to be an efficient and honest government servant. I too had set my mind on such a path. He used to tell me that business was an undesirable livelihood to take up and advised me to avoid friendship with the children of businessmen. I too felt no attraction for the world of business. The atmosphere in M.G. College was always stressful. There would be fights between students of different organizations almost every day. College would be closed for weeks together as a result of this. In my first year at the college, we had only eighty working days. This created a lack of security in the minds of students like me. I feared strikes.

Malayalam cine star Jagadish was my respected teacher in college. He had secured the first rank in the MCom examination and had been appointed as a lecturer. At that time, he used to participate in a programme titled *Ithalukal* on Akashavani. He had the ability to crack jokes and get along well with the students. Mohanlal, who later became a superstar in the cinema world, was also there as the final-year student.

Let me share here another significant memory that still remains shining in my mind. Literary competitions were being held in our college. A girl in my class had registered for the short-story competition. She told me about it on the day of the contest and requested me to go with her to the place where the competition was being held. As the place was far away, she was reluctant to go there alone. I decided to accompany her. However, only those who had registered their names could get into the hall. So, I would have to wait outside for her for more than an hour. Sensing my reluctance, she said, 'There is spot registration. Why don't you register now and get inside, Anu? Then you don't have to wait in the sun.'

That seemed to be a good idea. So I registered as a competitor and got inside. The theme for the short story was written on the black board: *Ormayute Deepanalangal* (The Flame of Memory). I started writing. Imagination and experience mingled seamlessly in my plot. Within the stipulated time of one hour, I handed in my creation. When the results came, I was awarded the first prize. In those days, creative efforts were much appreciated and such a victory would bring a lot of attention to the author. The appreciation and encouraging words from my teachers and friends demonstrated the truth in this.

There is another incident too during my college days which had the most unexpected outcome. A ten-day selection camp for badminton players was being conducted at the Valiyathura Indoor Stadium. The top ten players from our college were present. Only three players would be selected. I had just gone to see the stadium when I came to know about the selection trials. As the players started practising, it was found that one of them had not turned up. As his absence would interfere with the practice, the coach asked me to join them. I was ready to oblige and attended practice every day. When the final selection was announced, I was among the three players selected. It was a tremendous achievement for me to be selected for the college team. Many decades later, these experiences still bring joy and elation to my mind.

This was also the time when I suffered the most grievous loss in my life. I lost my father when I was in the second year of the degree course. His life was suddenly extinguished while he was at the pinnacle of his career.

The loss of my father and the resulting feeling of insecurity, combined with the turbid atmosphere in the college, made me averse to studies. I studied with my friends at home, but I had already decided not to appear for the examinations. The feeling that there was something more important than academic learning was gaining strength in my mind.

At this time, one of my friends, Ashok Varma, would come to my house for combined study. He was a brilliant student and took great pains to bring me back to my former studious self. He constantly persuaded me to do well in examinations, explaining subjects such as cost accounting and statistics in a way that made it easier for me to understand. He thus played an important part in my successfully completing my degree course.

After completing his course, Ashok went to Kolkata for higher studies, promising to meet me after becoming a cost accountant. I came to know that he secured a good job and continued to live in Kolkata.

Years later, Ashok's name came up before me while going through the applications for the post of cost accountant at Medimix. I recognized my old classmate and asked him to appear in person for the last and final round of interview.

That was when we met after a gap of several years. I had absolute faith in his competency and appointed him as head of the costing department. He worked in that position for ten years. As his health deteriorated, he had to stop working and unfortunately passed away soon after.

The strength of the college campus and the intensity of the youthful vigour create a special world for each student . . . one different from any other.

5

On to the Never-Ending Path

We are all wayfarers on an unending path. Some stage their entry while others depart. Some have a short tenure while others stay longer. This length refers to the longevity of human life. When compared with the lifespan of the earth and the innumerable beings on it, man, though boasting to be the master of all, has only a very short time to spend here. We have to build what we want within the time allotted to us. What we call progress has been the result of the work of great men. Today, we are on the threshold of being ruled by artificial intelligence, or AI. All that we enjoy has been made possible with the dedicated mind and sharp intelligence of the human race. No one can claim exclusive glory for any achievement; it can only be a part of a continuous flow. My life too is bound by this law. Let me now come to the story of how my life was fashioned to be endowed with substance and competence. We will have to traverse reality that bypasses our desires. Such was my fate—fate that made the once government job aspirant a successful businessman.

I enjoyed the pleasant and carefree life as a student of M.G. College, with everything for a high standard of life guaranteed as the son of a high-ranking government officer.

I had imbibed, even as a young man, the gentleness, humility and discipline that my father had taught by example. What I thought I lacked was freedom and appreciation, feelings that are common among all at that age. Youth is the time of rebelliousness too. But none had any complaints against me, only compliments came my way. My father sought only goodness, eschewing all that was unjust. His friends were from the higher echelons of society, including ministers. But his official position gave him the capacity to make laws to better the life of the ordinary fishermen and put them into practice. He made full use of it.

Once my father asked me to accompany him to the Palayam market to buy vegetables. It had never happened before. He drove us to the market. I was eighteen at that time and had just acquired my driving licence.

On reaching the market, my father handed me his wallet and the shopping bag and asked me to buy the vegetables. My heart brimmed with pride to see my father according me with adult responsibilities. I had become capable of doing things on my own! The door to the freedom I yearned for was about to open before me.

A greater surprise awaited me as I came back with the vegetables. 'You drive the car,' he said. My heart was filled with joy. My father was asking me to drive his car! My feelings at that moment were beyond words. What had come over him?

During that time, I sometimes felt that there was something troubling my father. But at that time, I did not have the maturity to understand the severity of his work responsibilities and the pressure from the higher-ups that he must have been enduring.

I drove my father home for the first time. I took out what I had bought and kept them all in place.

On reaching home, suddenly, my father started vomiting. We called the doctor, who was my friend's mother. She knew all of us very well. She examined my father and said, 'I think it is a heart attack. Take him to the hospital immediately.' We rushed him to the hospital. At the gate, my father got out and walked to the building. When I reached there after parking the car, my father was not there. He had been admitted in the ICU. At this age, I knew nothing about a heart attack or an ICU. I did not feel any fear or agitation; I had only that much of awareness about the world around me. I did not experience the emotions that anyone would have today on being informed that a beloved one has been admitted in the ICU. A young person at that time did not have the knowledge and awareness that youngsters have today. I had thought of hospitals, treatment and operations as things unrelated to me.

I called my brother-in-law Sudheer and informed him about the situation, and he soon joined me at the hospital. He was working as the forest range officer at Thiruvananthapuram at that time. My father's condition was slowly coming back to normal when the most unexpected thing happened. The air-conditioner in that room exploded with a loud noise. Even a small sound may endanger the life of cardiac patients in the ICU. It may lead to a rise in the rate of heart beats. The terrifying atmosphere created by this blast worsened my father's condition. Soon, he was shifted to the Medical College Hospital, where it was safer and more convenient and had the services of the specialists in the field.

The sudden hospitalization of my father created panic and uncertainty in his office also. He had a huge circle of friends and acquaintances. He was in charge of many important matters that had to be implemented on a daily basis. He had deep knowledge of the department that he headed. Inquiries about his condition came from innumerable places.

Dr Vijayaraghavan, a renowned specialist in cardiology, was in charge of his treatment. We waited outside, without sleep or food. On the second day our uncle, Dr Sidhan, came from Chennai. Some other relatives were also there. But on the third day, my father's condition worsened and he left us forever. He was only fifty-three at that time.

My mind started wandering like a kite snapped from its string. On hearing the news, Sidhan Uncle broke down and wept in front of all of us. We had all seen him as a strong, courageous man. Now he was crying uncontrollably at the loss we had suffered. That made me realize the depth of the pain and heartache the death of a dear one creates and the changes it leads to. I felt that I should console my uncle, and I did it. At that moment, I became a new person—a man capable of shouldering any responsibility.

News of the death of Sri Vasavan, director of fisheries, along with his photograph, appeared on the front page of all the newspapers on 18 March 1981. A huge crowd was present at the funeral. Words of consolation seemed not to touch my mind.

I had to take the decision on the place where my father was to be cremated. Shortly before, the electric crematorium had been opened in Thycaud. Many believed that burning the dead body using electricity was against religious norms. It had been difficult to get a body even for the inauguration. The authorities had to hunt for one to inaugurate the crematorium. I had heard about all this. I felt that my father, a humanitarian, who had no undue respect for rituals, should be cremated at that crematorium. Thus, there was a deviation from the age-old custom in the first important decision I made. Some of my relatives were not happy about my decision.

Though his physical body was reduced to ashes in the crematorium, my father continues to sleep peacefully in the silken bed of my heart; I often sing lullabies for him.

Many people gave me small amounts of money for the cremation and other rituals connected with it. Sidhan Uncle comforted me by promising to send some money across every month.

I was worried about my family's expenses. I went through all the cupboards at home. There was not much to be found there. There was nothing left in the bank either. Repayment of the loan taken for the car was still pending. Now I had to take the initiative and complete the remaining responsibilities. The only hope lay in the amount to be got from the Life Insurance Corporation (LIC). So, I started the process for getting the amount that should come to the dependents on the death of the insurer. It was then that I realized the difficulty in getting what rightfully belonged to us. The series of events that followed showed how callous and insolent officers can be.

I had to visit many offices many times to get the death certificate and to get a mistake rectified in the one issued to us. The same routine had to be followed for the heir-ship certificate. Every time I went to an office, I would be sent back with instructions to come another day. Some of them insisted that my mother be present before them. The realization that an officer is more of a royal handyman dawned on me at that time. I wondered about what other laymen would have to suffer since I was still able to seek the benefits for a loved one who occupied a high position in the bureaucratic world. The government offices I visited were epitomes of arrogance and depravity.

The most unjust treatment came from the LIC office at Pattom, Thiruvananthapuram. We had submitted all the papers the officers had asked for and were waiting to get the money that was rightfully due to us. But what happened that day surpassed the limits of decency.

The LIC office had kept my mother's application for release of money in abeyance for six months. Then they demanded that she must produce certificates from three people, who were not related to us, who had attended my father's funeral. This was more than what I could bear. My blood boiled at the unreasonable demand, and I raised my voice. I threw all the papers I had brought with me at the face of the person who had made this demand and stormed out. If the walls of the office could speak, they would recount what happened that day. As I walked out, our last hope of some sustenance had been buried. But miraculously, the cheque for the amount due to us from the LIC arrived by post two days later.

The attitude of the officers has changed considerably since those days. The main reason for it is the stiff competition that came in the wake of privatization. Now one does not have to wait for the mercy of the officers at the banks. They come home looking for customers.

In another instance, I have suffered from Bharat Sanchar Nigam Limited (BSNL) officers. Back then, BSNL had the monopoly on telephones.

The telephone at home had been allotted to my father in his official capacity. There is a law that allows the heirs to get the phone if an officer in a higher position passes away. But when we applied for it, the officers asked us to return the telephone. I had to go to many offices many times to get we had the right to have.

In my office in Chennai, there were more than fifty land phone connections. In those days, there was the custom of giving gifts to the officers of the BSNL on festive occasions such as Deepavali. The intention was to make sure that we got their help to keep all the phones working.

One day, a group of people arrived at the office to see me. As they had not taken prior appointment for a meeting, the staff at the reception was asked to find out who they were. I was informed that they were officers from BSNL, including some engineers. They had come to give me a present. I had been declared as the Most Privileged Customer! At last, the mountain had come to Mohammed!

Such changes were caused by the stiff competition in all spheres as well as the adoption of international standards in judging the quality of a product or service.

After my father's death, the attempt to collect the arrears on his income tax caused us some difficulty. Threats, in the form of demand notices, kept arriving. The amount was small, but we were not in a position to pay that. I went to their office. I asked why they had not collected it by reducing the amount from the salary every month. I went to the extent of asking them why they were acting without any compassion, threatening to collect money from someone who were evidently in a difficult state.

These experiences with government offices made me realize that bureaucracy is not concerned about our losses and difficulties. To take life forward, one must have a good regular income. I had some liabilities to clear. I also had to get my sister married.

My first priority was to find a regular income. My brother-in-law Sudheer became my guide in that venture. He had a Matador van with a seating capacity of seven. It had not become very common at that time. He gave me that vehicle to find a livelihood. So, I became a taxi driver!

I got many customers. Acquaintances extended a helping hand. I took the teachers to the college and back home. As families could travel comfortably in it, I got such trips too. Many people booked my van for Saturdays and Sundays. There were more demands than what I could handle. Some people called me on the telephone, but there was nobody to attend to it.

Amma had not yet come back to her normal self. She was still depressed and in tears very often.

As bookings for my Matador increased, I realized that I had to take steps to meet the demand. I had only that one vehicle. It was not enough to cater to all those who called me. As it was my source of income, I did not want to reject the requests for bookings. So, I appointed a driver on a commission basis to run the trips.

Now I could attend to the calls for bookings. Also, I could arrange vehicles from other agencies for all the bookings and get commission on that. This was how I learned how to run a business successfully through delegation.

I could get up to Rs 10,000 per month from this. My father's basic salary was just Rs 1864.

I was a college student and a taxi driver at the same time. I could not attend classes regularly. I begged my teachers to mark my attendance. As they were aware of my position, they obliged. Some of them must have remembered adages that spoke about the transient nature of wealth and position in human life, when they saw my transformation. Strikes also helped as classes were not held regularly because of them.

It was April 1982. I was to appear for the final examination of BCom then. We had study holidays in

February and March. I did a lot of business at that time; my van was running almost incessantly. I was also representing my college in inter-collegiate shuttle badminton tournaments at that time.

During this time, Sidhan Uncle came to our house to take rest for some time.

Waves of love and care engulf my mind at the mere mention of my uncle's name. I cannot define who and what he was to me; I would rather try describing who all and what all he had been to me.

He was my uncle, my partner in the world of entertainment, my father-in-law, managing director of Medimix and an eminent doctor, but beyond all these mundane descriptions, we shared a deeper relationship of the hearts. There was love, respect, concern and care in that bond.

This visit laid the foundation for this relationship between us.

Dr V.P. Sidhan was one who created history that broke the limitations of time.

He was a student of GCIM & DM&S* at the Kilpauk Medical College, Chennai, in 1950. Those who successfully completed this course were allowed to practise both allopathy and Ayurveda. He was the son of Dr V.K. Padmanabhan of the Cholayil family. He wanted his son also to practise allopathic medicine like him. The son was a good student and excelled in acting and other such activities too. This earned him a vast array of friends from all walks of life.

---

* GCIM and DM&S: Government College of Integrated Medicine and Doctor of Medicine and Surgery

Dr Sidhan was driven by the enthusiasm to achieve rare distinctions in the world of medicine. He studied the tomes on Ayurveda with diligence. Ayurveda, the *veda* (holy word) on *ayus* (life) is based on the medicinal plants described in the different ancient books. Sixty-seven medicinal plants have been mentioned in the ancient work, Rig Veda, eighty-one in the Yajur Veda, 290 in the Atharva Veda, 600 in the Sushruta Samhita, 700 in the Chakara Samhita and 700 in the Ashtanga Hrudaya. Dr Sidhan studied all these and sought to help his patients with complete cure of their ailments.

On completing his studies, he was appointed as an allopathic doctor at the railway hospital in Perambur. It was a major hospital, with many departments, including facilities for heart surgeries in those days.

He soon became a busy and popular doctor. He found that most of the patients who approached him suffered from skin diseases. Ordinary railway employees, called *khalasi*s, suffered most from this. The usual chemical formulae prescribed for this seemed to have no effect on these men. So he felt that he should find another medicine for this.

His studies led him to prepare *viprathi*, which his ancestors used to prescribe for skin diseases. He made a new medicine with the ingredients used in that preparation and gave it to his patients. The results were nothing short of phenomenal. Its fame spread and demand too grew. Even other doctors wanted that oil. This led Dr Sidhan into thinking of using the same ingredients and making a soap without losing its curative power. That would prove beneficial to more people, and he would get a chance to take the ancient knowledge available in his family to the larger market.

The first soap was made at home in the kitchen. He was helped by his wife, Soubhagyam. When he was sure that the soap had the same beneficial effects as the oil viprathi, he kept it for sale in the medical shop near his house. Soon he expanded the market by making it available in more medical shops in Tamil Nadu. 'Recommended by Doctors' was the catchphrase that helped in the sales. It was handmade without using electricity.

He opened a small factory at Perambur to increase production. Dr Pavithran, who had been a close friend from their college days, suggested the name Medimix—A Mixture of Medicines—and that name was given to the product.

As Dr Sidhan had to go to the hospital early in the morning, his wife was made in-charge of manufacturing the soap. As those who used it once came back for it again, they had to make more soaps. They had to employ some workers for that. Some workers were brought to Perambur from Kerala. Though the company gave them all help and care, they were not satisfied. They created trouble about the quality of the food provided to them and formed a trade union, eventually going on strike. The company had to be shut down. The workers did not stop at that. They started threatening and abusing Dr Sidhan. Posters threatening his life appeared on the walls of the factory. Efforts were made to arrive at an amicable solution, but all those attempts were defeated. Dr Sidhan found himself in a situation where he could not continue with what he had started.

Dr Sidhan ended coming to our house. He wanted time to think of a plan to overcome the difficult situation and find a way to start production again. It was also a chance for him to be with his sister, who had become a widow recently. He felt that he too would gain by her presence near him.

That visit proved to be an important turning point in my life too.

6

Single Room to Corporate Office

'If you wish to reach the highest, begin at the lowest.'
—Publilius Syrus

A New Dawn

I got a long letter from my uncle after he returned to Chennai. That put me in a dilemma. He wanted me to shift to Madras and take up the business he once started. I could not take a hasty decision on that. I was entitled to get a job in the government service under the dying-in-harness scheme as I had become a graduate, and my father had died while in service. Many of those who heard about the suggestion did not support the idea of leaving the security of a government job.

But I took a firm decision. There were mainly two things that helped me in this regard. One was the self-confidence I had gained in doing business while still a student. The other was the bitter experience I had encountered at the many government offices that I was forced to visit in order to get the legal heir certificate after the death of my father.

That letter and the decision I took on that changed my whole life.

15 May 1983

I reached Chennai that day. The language and the culture there were alien to me. I had given up a cushy government job on my own. Whatever knowledge I had about realizing a business dream had been gained from books. But bookish knowledge will not directly just translate into success. My lack of practical experience was a real drawback.

My uncle had high hopes about me succeeding. That hope, alone, was my strength. As he had been transferred, he had to leave for Madurai. With the stethoscope, he carried a portable typewriter with him on this trip to send type-written instructions to his nephew, who had now taken charge of the company. He would send me instructions on what I should do each day, whom I should meet, how to select the raw materials, how to maintain quality of the product and many more such aspects of the business. As he had not practised speed typing, he had to type it out using one finger. I would learn the instructions carefully and follow them accurately. I would call him to give the report. If I had kept those letters, it would have been a valuable reference book for management students. I could have named it 'Letters from Dr V.P. Sidhan to Anoop', reminiscent of the collection of letters that Jawaharlal Nehru wrote from the jail to his daughter Indira: 'Letters from a Father to His Daughter'.

As I stepped into the depths of the duty I had undertaken, realization dawned on me that running a business was not a bed of roses. But I would never run away from the difficulties before me. That was not what a man would do. I prepared my mind to meet any challenge. For this, I owe much to some of my colleagues. One of them was K.H.S. Manian, who joined the company as an ordinary staff and retired as the president after a service of forty-seven years. K.V. Prakash, who served as administrative officer and general manager, was another. He is not alive now. C.R. Vinayachandran, who was a personal assistant to Dr Sidhan, is yet another of them. He used to cycle to Dr Sidhan's residence early in the morning so that he could get his instructions before Dr Sidhan left for the hospital. Later he was elevated to a higher post. P. Mohanan, who was also PA to Dr Sidhan, is another name to be mentioned. It is through all of them also that I learned business and put those lessons into practice. To this day we continue to retain a good relationship.

One name that features prominently in this list is that of P.K. Joseph, the auditor of the company. He was our first auditor and we were his first client. Even now we remain the foremost customer of his company. I learnt a lot from him and he learnt a lot from our company. The warmth of our relationship has not faded to this day.

I cannot leave out D. Rajendran, who looked after the production of the soap covers, notices, calendars and other printed matter from the very beginning. He was the agent of a prominent company in Sivakashi. Later he rose to a very high position in that field. The secret of his success was his readiness to adapt to the advancing technology in printing.

One day, we were travelling through Karnataka looking for unadulterated coconut oil when we met Kumar, a mill owner in Tipthur Arisikere. He was facing a major setback at that time. He had not been able to pay back the loan he had taken from the bank to establish the oil mill. Now the bank had started proceedings against him and he could not open his mill. The bank was making arrangements to confiscate his property. We promised to help him if he would assure us long term, loyal service. He agreed to it and he was able to reopen the mill.

This benefited both of us. They have kept the word given at that time to this day. Their company, Ravi Industries, has grown more than Medimix. They are the major distributors of coconut oil in south India now.

We had to look for coconut oil from Karnataka rather than Kerala because the producers in Kerala were reluctant to enter into any long-term agreement. As of 2021–22, Kerala was trailing behind in the third place in the production of coconut oil. While other states have got coconut plantations, Kerala does not have them. It is high time that people changed the usual complaint that coconut cultivation does not yield any profit.

Medimix is made in the traditional way. First, the hot soap mixture is poured into a cooling box. After five days, the moulds are cut into slabs. These are then cut into bars. The thin bars that remain in place of the mould is cut into bars and recycled. The idea that these could be made into mini soaps for use in the hotels was successfully implemented. As these smaller soaps had the same quality of the bigger ones in the market, the hotel owners and their customers accepted them happily. The demand for the mini soaps increased and they also helped us in introducing our product to those who stayed in hotels.

To begin with, we wanted at least a hundred hotels to use it. But the number of those who wanted it increased day by day and we could not meet the demand with the leftover bars. So we started producing mini soaps. Today, most of the hotels in India give Medimix soap for the use of those who stay in their rooms. We have come to understand that if Medimix was not provided in the rooms, guests would recommend buying that. Now we have a factory manufacturing only soaps that need to be supplied to the hotels.

When we first went out to the market with soaps weighing 18 g, the wholesale dealers used to make fun of us. Some of them vehemently expressed their opinion that small soaps will not be accepted. But a large number of travellers, construction workers, those who work in hotels and many others from different walks of life accepted it and we had to have a factory exclusively for that. In famous tourist spots like Courtallam Waterfalls, visitors still enjoy a Medimix bath.

Many were the impediments we had to face even in the face of progress. On several occasions, we had to struggle to find enough money to pay the salary to the employees. There were occasions when I waited at the bank at the end of the month to see if enough money was coming into our account. When there was a shortfall, we would call the distributors and request their help. Their co-operation has been most helpful. I can say with a sense of pride that in the fifty years of our business history, there was no occasion when salary could not be paid. Our custom is to pay it on the fifth of every month; if that was a holiday, payment would be made on the previous day. Times when there was not enough money in hand and we had to pawn our gold to furnish it, are still fresh in my mind. If I can write this today, it is only because I was ready to see a crisis as a challenge and sought ways to surmount it.

I have witnessed the fall of many companies that came up with a lot of fanfare during this time. What led to their untimely exit are the lack of proper planning and money for capital investment. There is also the false belief that doing business is an easy job—a belief that they gather on seeing the success of some other entrepreneurs. Most of those who venture into the world of business are unaware that it requires a lot of thought, supported by an ardent desire to succeed. Sound and ethical strategies are essential for the success of any enterprise. Many carry the false impression that if there is enough money, anyone can do business. Money is only one among the innumerable factors needed for the success of a business.

I had the terrifying experience of having to appear in court and receive punishment for the work I was doing. That taught me the valuable lesson that ignorance of law is not an excuse. When you start a business, it is essential to be aware of the rules and regulations connected with it. This should be seen as a lesson for those who are starting new ventures. Till 1985, it was not necessary to take a licence for making soaps. But when making of soaps was also included under the law for drugs and cosmetics and once the law came into force, a licence became mandatory for making soaps. Medimix Ayurvedic Soap also came under it.

The government had announced this in advance for the information of all those who were concerned with it. But we did not come to know of it. We had not entrusted any one with the task of bringing to our notice the rules and regulations regarding the running of the company and make necessary modifications. Those who were actually involved in the running of the company did not pay much attention to all that. So we had to pay a hefty price for it.

Officers came to our factory for inspection and demanded to see the drug licence. As we did not possess it, they locked up the premises and sealed all the equipment, raw materials and the finished product that had been packed for distribution.

This was a shock for me and the members of my family. It weakened us both physically and mentally. All this would not have happened if we had taken the licence which would cost just Rs 60. But it taught us an important lesson. Ignorance of a change in law was a major lapse on our own part. Making Ayurvedic soap without a licence was liable for punishment with imprisonment. This was specifically mentioned in the charge sheet submitted by the department of drugs and cosmetics in the court. The days that followed were tension-filled, with sleepless nights. Then at last, the case was taken up for consideration and the orders were passed. The judge made a reference to the efforts of a young man to run a business with all good intentions. The punishment was for me to stand as a prisoner in the court premises till the end of proceedings for that day. The case was the last item for the day and the orders were also passed, just as the court was about to close for the day. So the rule that was to punish me, in turn, came to save me here. The judge who made matters favourable for me is nothing short of God for me. The memory of what seemed a mountain in front of me and terrified me for long but ended as a gentle pat, is still fresh in memory.

In the initial stages, we, Dr Sidhan, his son Pradeep, I and other officers used to go around on cycles with the bags containing soap packets for sale. One such journey will never fade from my memory. I used to board the Yercaud Express every day for Salem and go to Athur, 50 km away, by bus. Taking a cycle on rent from there I would go to the remote village of Narasimhapuram. Our soap factory was in a small tile-roofed house there. Dr Chacko, a friend of Dr Sidhan, had found this place for the factory. There were small manufacturing units at Chengalpattu and Poonamallee too.

In 1983, I was sent to Mumbai to work for the distribution of our soap. Dr Vijayan, a classmate of Dr Sidhan, had asked me to come there. I stayed in his house at Ambarnath.

I would travel from there early in the morning by electric train to VT Station, which was 75 km away. The distributor for Medimix had his shop near the VT Station. My assistant and I would take two bags packed with soaps and travel in the crowded trains. At each station, we would go to the nearby shops carrying the heavy bags and try to sell the soap. I had to face abusive behaviour from shopkeepers many a time. Some had even thrown the soap at me deriding me as 'Madrasi-wallah'. My inability to handle their language efficiently was a barrier in communication. I depended on the few Hindi words and expressions I had learnt while I was an NCC cadet. But there was an incident which came as a sequel to this, a rather pleasant surprise.

I was in the office at Chennai that day. I got a call asking for an appointment for the caller to see me. When the person introduced himself, I was shocked. It was the owner of the huge business empire, Adi Godrej, calling me from Chola Sheraton hotel. I went to meet him. I was meeting, in person, a man I always looked up to. Whatever obscure ideas I had about the owner of a corporate company were shattered after this meeting. He had called me knowing that Medimix soap was selling well in most of the shops near the railway stations in Bombay. We talked about the manufacturing and sale of soaps. The Godrej company had developed and brought into the market an ingredient needed for the manufacturing of soaps. He had called me to introduce that product to me and requested me to recommend buying that ingredient in our factories. I met him once again at a function of the All-India Soap

Manufacturers' Association, sponsored by Godrej. The people who had come to attend the meeting were standing in a queue, with lunch coupons in hand. At the end of the long queue was Adi Godrej. I was immensely impressed by his patience, humility and the dignified way in which he mingled with those around him.

Our customers increased in numbers and manufacturing and distribution grew with it. So we thought of relocating our office to a more convenient place. I went to look at a flat in an apartment of four in Chennai. A very prominent person in the film world lived in one of the flats. Coming to know of my intention, he advised me, 'This place does not auger well for the occupants. Don't take it.' He then took me to his flat. A heap of film roles lay in a corner of one room. 'These are films that I directed. Now I have to live by selling these as scrap.' He felt that the presence of the planets being in the wrong position for this flat was responsible for the fate of his films.

He told me that the others in that building were also facing similar problems. But I took the flat as I had no belief in such astrological matters. I thought of the many enterprises started with good intentions, going to ruin because of the belief in superstitions and improper customs. I told the gentleman that I was taking it temporarily for six months. Soon the other occupants left the place and we added those areas also into our office. I know many who have destroyed their life with too much belief in horoscope, numerology and Vaastu. I want to prove from my own experience that one should depend on one's own intelligence and logic in all matters. It is time we stopped pawning our intelligence for superstitious beliefs.

The growth of our enterprise from one room in the house to a multistorey corporate office was not made on a path strewn with petals. Many were the impediments faced on this journey. Many unforgettable incidents mark this transition. One of the most interesting is the journey in search of the attractive perfume that is unique to the Medimix soap.

Each use must be a sensation. The smell of the product has a lot to do in this. The quality and the smell must last even to the last sliver. We wanted perfumes that would not hamper the medicinal quality of the soap till the end and will be attractive to people of all ages under all climatic conditions. We searched far and wide for that.

We approached many manufacturers of perfumes. None of them were ready even to meet us. We were not allowed to go to their laboratories. At each place, we were given a strip dipped in a particular perfume. We had to smell it and decide if it was something we wanted. This was not an easy process. As each smell was different, it could not be done in haste. But as it was essential for us to get the right smell, we went on continuing with it and soon reached a stage where we could distinguish one from the other. I would say that my nose and my brain started coordinating perfectly. Soon, I established a close affinity with things through smell.

But I did not get a smell that was suitable for an Ayurvedic soap which had not been used before. I continued with my search and studies. That led me to three companies. I started an effort to make a new perfume with the perfumers in those companies in their laboratories. This effort lasted for more than a year. By then we had prepared three herbal perfumes suitable for Medimix.

Now we had to choose one of them. We were in a dilemma like those in a reality show where the judges had to choose one from those in the elimination round. It was not easy to eliminate any of them. They had cooperated with us so well, leading to an unforgettable indebtedness. When we conducted a market survey, all three had gained good ratings. Mentally, I had become so close to all three companies that it was impossible to reject any one of them. I awarded them marks on the basis of the obligation and love I had for them.

My mind seemed to tell me that if the three perfumes were mixed in the ratio of the marks I had allotted them, it would yield a good result. I jumped with joy, feeling like Newton when the apple had fallen on his head.

I was reminded of the saying that suggested the *sulaimani* tea in an *Ustad* hotel is so tasty as it has *mohabat* (love) of the maker mixed with it.

The unique smell of the Medimix soap, which no one can duplicate, is the result of the combination of great love and care. I got the help of Rajesh Shenoy, Shajahan and Jayan Pillai in achieving this.

Let me share with you a pleasant experience I had while looking for a suitable perfume. This happened in Amsterdam, the Netherlands. Dr Sidhan and I were visiting a perfume factory there. We had taken an appointment to meet the executives of the factory.

We decided to choose the appropriate dress for the meeting. We felt that as is usual in international business meetings, we should be formally dressed in suits. That is considered the best attire as it will reflect the position and dignity of the wearer.

The officers of the company gave us a hearty welcome with bouquets of flowers. They must have heard of the Indian belief that the guest should be respected like God. What struck us was the way our hosts were dressed. They were in casuals, short trousers and T-shirts. We felt at odds, dressed formally in suits.

The preliminary meeting was over. Now there was a dinner meeting. Before going for that, Dr Sidhan said to them, 'We have to go to our rooms to take our medicine.'

When we reached the room, we started laughing, thinking of the incongruity of our suit and shoes with their casual wear.

We had no medicines to take at that time. It was only an excuse to change our dress. We removed the suit and got into T-shirts. We both had worn different costumes in plays and films to suit the mood and the occasion and now we had to do the same for work. After checking our appearance once again in the mirror we went back to the place of our meeting. Both the parties had a shock when they looked at each other. They were in suits! They had changed while we had gone to 'take the medicine'.

Our company leads in the best utilization of human resources. We find the people suited for running the company in the best way; we train them and entrust them with the work. Let me tell you how I came to appoint the man who worked in the technology department for many years. In those days, there were many factors that controlled the production. We were using wood burners in factories. That naturally led to smoke that caused a lot of discomfort for those inside the factory. As the fire had to be kept burning with someone blowing into it, production was limited. We were looking for some technology to overcome this.

One day, I heard somebody talking loudly near my house. A middle-aged man was speaking angrily with someone. The person he was berating was the Honourable President of India, K.R. Narayanan. I went to him to find out the reason for his anger. His son had written a poem in English and sent it to the President. The President realized the value of what the boy had created and wanted to meet him. So he invited him to Rashtrapati Bhavan. This rare and unique invitation that his son had received angered the father.

'Who will give him the money to go to Delhi? Is it right to invite children like this?' he went on asking.

I consoled him and he finally calmed down.

I talked to him about the importance of such an invitation and how it was a huge recognition for his son's ability. I made him see that what his son had got was an unusual honour. As I went on talking to him, he started speaking about his own special skills.

He spoke proudly about the experiments he had conducted successfully even though he had studied only up to the Class VIII. He told me that he had made a device that would increase the speed of a cycle. I understood that he had a 'mechanical mind' who could use technology in a practical manner. I was thinking of procuring some machines that would help in increasing production. I had already visited many engineering companies with no avail. Later, I talked to him about the details of production in my factory and the urgent need to increase production. He listened to it all and gave me a reply indicating that it was just child's play for him. He had only one question for me: 'What will you give me if I make a suitable machine for you? Will you get me a new cycle?'

I agreed.

I took him to our factory at Madhavaram. He understood what was needed and made a smokeless oven which made production easier. With that, we had overcome the main difficulty in increasing production. He was indeed a jewel from the dustbin. Realizing his expertise, we made him a managing partner in a new company for developing new machines.

In the place of the new cycle that had been promised in the beginning, we gave him a new car. Both his sons were brilliant, and we helped in getting both of them a good education. They are in esteemed positions outside India today.

His dedicated service of over twenty-five years helped a lot in the development of the company. This man is George Philip, who retired as the head of the company that manufactures machineries. At eighty, he continues to be active and in good health. He is one who can rightfully be acclaimed as a 'star performer'.

Medimix is handmade, without the aid of electricity or power. There are definite advantages of such a process. Consumers like fresh handmade products as the use of traditional methods helps them feel an emotional attachment to the product. This is similar to how we always believe that the chutney made by our mothers on the stone grinder with their own hands tastes better than anything made with an electric mixer grinder.

Another great advantage is that such products do not attract any tax.

We tried many experiments to increase production without using electricity. Most of the innovative practices introduced by Philip, who was an employee, at that time were highly successful.

One such innovation was to keep the vehicle on a ramp and use the natural force of gravity to make the oil, the raw material in the manufacture of soap, flow down through a pipe. A revolutionary change was achieved when we started using the cutting machine that could be worked by hand which enabled us to cut hundreds of soaps at the same time. By incorporating all these methods, we were able to produce more than ten lakh cakes of soaps of different variety each day.

Truth is we could do it faster using machines. But we did not have the huge capital to buy the machines in those days.

Many people were curious to know how we handled the workers. The answer is simple: We have always done our best for the welfare of our workers. We employ the people of the village where the factory is situated, thus empowering locals, especially women. The power women get from being employed and the support from the company has helped many achieve a respectable position in society. After marriage, many of our women employees made their husbands stay in the wives' houses instead of staying in the husbands' houses, as was the custom.

We want the families of each of our employees to be self-sufficient. Their children must get good education and high-ranking jobs. We have been able to fulfill these wishes with our timely intervention and support. There are many doctors, engineers, IT professionals and others coming from the families of our company, working in different parts of the world. Our policy is that the children of our workers should not come seeking employment as workers in our factories.

We want the locality also to improve along with the workers. We ask the workers what they want from us to improve the condition of the place where the factories function. Some ask for toilets. In this regard, we have constructed tanks for the storage of drinking water and community halls on the request of the workers.

We have efficiently utilized corporate social responsibility (CSR) funding and made various schemes for the welfare of our workers. We wish that there would be no family without a house of its own. We do our utmost to realize this dream. This has gone a long way in cementing our relationship with our workers.

7

The Birth of 'Sanjeevanam': My Thoughts on Healthy Living

Nothing happens without a cause. When new ideas sprout in your mind and they grow and yield results, we start thinking deeply about why they happened. I take interest in varied aspects of life and I lead a happy life while being intimately connected with society. My personal life and public life are so merged that one cannot be separated from the other. I feel that my life illustrates the wisdom in the saying 'Man proposes; God disposes.' I wanted to be an engineer. My father wanted me to be in government service. When I took commerce and later decided to pursue BCom, there was no change in the aim. Looking back, I feel that the course I studied in college built the steps that led me to the vast ocean of the world of commerce. I have realized that there is something beyond and above our desires which controls and builds up the opportunities we get and the circumstances of our life. The stories of those who have achieved significant success in life prove this to be true.

People of different spheres view me differently as a person. For some, I am an industrialist. For others, I am a producer of films. Yet others see me as one who acts in plays and in films. Those who are involved in philanthropic activities see me as one of them. I sometimes indulge in over-analysing this concept.

For your personality to grow, it is essential that you make self-assessments at least twice a year. This will help you find out your shortcomings and defects, and also cure them, thus ensuring you lead a glorious life. Today, when I make this suggestion to society, I remember with gratitude my friend who taught me to do this many years ago. He was K.K. Rajendran, popularly known as Chakyar Rajan. I never had a friend who could talk and make speeches with so much of wit and wisdom. He was a management consultant in Bombay. The first time I met him was at a shooting location in Andhra. I had gone there for the shooting of a serial for Doordarshan titled *Oridathth Oridathth* (directed by Raghavan). Our friendship lasted till the end of his life.

Chakyar is a surname of a sub-sect of the Hindu community in Kerala. A Chakyar had the right to criticize, in public, all the immorality and incongruities in society, presenting everything with a touch of humour. In earlier times, Chakyar Koothu was a performing art patronized by the temples in Kerala. While reciting some Puranic story, the Chakyar would bring in examples from the present-day life. The Chakyar could openly state what another man dared not speak in public: a system similar to satire in English literature. Rajan had become a 'Chakyar' by virtue of his innate sense of humour.

He demonstrated in equal measure his expertise in the fields of arts and in management. The relationship between the two of us later led to our families developing close ties with each other. This friendship extended to my uncle Dr Sidhan and brother-in-law Pradeep too. Both Dr Sidhan

and Rajan were theatre fans as the field of drama was close
to their hearts. This interest was strong enough to make
him take a flight to Chennai for a rehearsal camp.

Rajan's expertise in management helped in regularizing
the running of the Medimix company. He guided us in
different aspects of management like convening the board
meetings, initiating disciplinary actions and in putting
into practice all the ideas that came from discussions and
analysis, for the development of the company. He prepared
the minutes of the meetings according to the relative
importance of different matters. I am sure that it helped
a lot in our progress. Our relationship grew beyond the
business world, and we found ourselves discussing various
matters almost every day. We used to talk for a long time
over the phone. I came to see his ability in presenting things
in a dramatic way while attending a felicitation meeting
at Thrissur. The meeting was held under the leadership of
Dr Ramanathan, of the Sitaram Ayurveda products. The
words that Rajan uttered in introducing me to the audience
are still etched in my memory.

'I was surprised to hear you speak so highly about
Anoop. My experience is different from that. When he first
saw me, he tried to murder me with lethal weapons. I had
to run for my life. This is still fresh in my memory.'

After a pause, he continued, 'I was talking about my
experience in acting in a serial in which he was acting as
the commander in chief of the army.'

I was introduced to Rajan by actor and film director
Raghavan. He has a unique ability to present any subject
in a special way. He suggested the name 'Sanjeevanam' for
my Ayurvedic hospital.

I had already made plans for establishing a treatment
centre where naturopathy, yoga and Ayurveda could

be incorporated. My family's Ayurvedic roots of over 400 years gave me the self-confidence to begin such an establishment. From personal experience, I realized that age-old traditional knowledge often proved to be more effective than modern medical learning.

The Inter-Club Badminton Tournament was going on at the Chennai Towers Club. There were five teams and five events. When the fifth team fell short of one player, they approached me. I had not thought of participating in the tournament that year, but I agreed to oblige the team. It was the third game, and our team was about to be defeated in a closely contested match. I decided to give up the refined strokes taught by the coach and started playing in my own way. My opponents were completely overshadowed and we won the match. But in the middle of our victory celebrations, I collapsed because my hip was cramping. As I was being carried out by my friends, our victory was being announced over the mike. Towers Club had won the tournament and a cash award of Rs 10,000 was given. The amount was sponsored by Medimix. The knowledge that I had played so hard for my own money douched my spirits slightly, but the excruciating pain pushed all other thoughts off my mind. Then came the long period of treatment. Many eminent doctors examined me. They diagnosed the problem being related to the disk and suggested surgery as the only option for relief. For an active person like me, being confined to my room was unbearable. I couldn't walk or turn my body. The pain was unbearable. Many people made inquiries about my condition; some came in person while others called me on the phone. The doctors had advised twenty-four-hour bed rest. But remaining idle was not a part of my nature. When Baiju, son of Gokulam Gopalan (Gopalettan for me), came to hear about it, he

made a suggestion. There was a *vaidyan*, or physician, in
T. Nagar called Bhadrayya. 'He may be able to offer some
relief,' he suggested.

I firmly believed in the dictum that a quack is more
likely to kill than cure. I could not go beyond the opinion
of the highly qualified doctors. Still Baiju persisted. 'Allow
him just to see you,' he requested me.

With half a mind, I agreed to that. 'You need not
take any medicines. Just come to my place at 4 o'clock
in the morning,' he said. The next day I was there at the
appointed time. He checked my pulse and said that there
was nothing seriously wrong with me. Then he started
running his hand over various parts of my body—poking,
pressing and so on. He used a stone pestle to press and rub
at certain points. Then he asked me to walk slowly. I did so
to my own utter surprise. I had arrived there a few minutes
ago in a condition where I could not move my body. But
now I was walking! Wonder of wonders! He told me that
there was no need to take rest. He suggested some simple
exercises to be done every day. I had to go there only two
or three times after that. This experience showed me that it
was not only modern medicine that could come to the help
of the patient; traditional medicine also had a significant
role to play in this field. I follow the exercises suggested by
Bhadrayya even today. Many officers in the Indian Police
Service (IPS) and similar ranks approach Bhadrayya for
help with their ailments. This man from Andhra continues
to be busy with his treatment to this day.

I have understood the importance of food in alternative
medical treatment. There was a hotel in Thiruvananthapuram
that followed Mahatma Gandhi's dictum—that food is
medicine—and offered food made with ingredients that
did not contain harmful substances. We could get items

made without using oil, masala and chemical substances.
I came to know about this hotel from Gopalettan. I talked
to the owner Surendran about the various aspects of the
establishment and indicated my deep interest in it. I was
more interested in providing healthy food in our capital
city than in making a lot of profit from it.

In those days, one of my relatives had a hotel at
Palayam in Thiruvananthapuram, named Town Hotel. It
was a well-known establishment. As it was near the MLA
Hostel, many leaders of political parties used to come there
often. With only very limited facilities available for stay
for the people who came to Thiruvananthapuram, many of
the visitors who arrived by bus in the night used to sleep
in the limited comforts available at Town Hotel. I bought
that property. In partnership with Surendran, I started a
nature hotel named Kadalivanam. Soon there were many
hotels with the same name functioning in various parts of
the city. I talked to Chakyar Rajan about these spurious
Kadalivanams. He pointed out the necessity of establishing
a brand name of our own. Sanjeevanam was a result of that
suggestion.

Sanjeevanam was started in Chennai with the intention
of providing Ayurveda, naturopathy and Yoga under one
roof. Along with natural products, food and paintings
were also available for sale there. This was inaugurated by
Gaanagandharvan Padmasree Yesudas. My acquaintance
with *Dasettan* for many years made this possible. Soon
a branch was opened at Adyar. The renowned musician
Sri M. Balamuralikrishna inaugurated that branch and
visited it for treatment too. The branch at Nungambakkam
was inaugurated by the famous violinist Kunnakudi
Vaidyanathan. Music director Deva opened the branch at
the Andhra Club. Sanjeevanam started functioning in cities

such as Ahmadabad and Pune too. The Mogappair branch
was declared open by P. Susheela, one of the greatest and
best-known playback singers in India. But soon it was
impossible to run all the branches with the same standard
of perfection. The lack of employees who were devoted
to the special nature of the institution was also another
reason that made it impossible to continue.

Preliminary work had commenced for a branch of
Sanjeevanam at Sharjah in the UAE as it was considered
to have great potential as a place to demonstrate the
goodness and curative power of Ayurveda to the world.
But unfortunately, that had to be closed the day it was
opened. Doctors who used Ayurvedic medicines in their
treatment in the UAE had to pass a special examination.
Even those who had qualified as Ayurvedic doctors in
India found it difficult to pass this examination. Getting
permission for the use of all the Ayurvedic preparations
was also impossible. When we started the establishment
there, the health club in one of the five-star hotels in
Dubai had been granted permission to offer Ayurvedic
treatment. I visited that health club to see the type of
treatment offered there. That place gave me a surprise.
The cleanliness, orderliness and the equipment used there
were of an international standard. That was beyond my
imagination. This changed my perception. I would never
be able to come up to this level of perfection. So I decided
to start an Ayurvedic hospital of that standard in Kerala
and run it successfully before venturing out to the Gulf. It
was with this concept that I came to establish Sanjeevanam
at Ernakulam. I decided to set up a centre that would
create a new concept about Ayurveda in the minds of the
foreigners. For that, the centre should keep up to the level of
cleanliness and treatment available in world-class hospitals

and also find a means to avoid the smell associated with Ayurvedic medicines. The land which had been bought for building an apartment complex was chosen for the project at Pallikkara in Kakkanad, Ernakulam. With my son-in-law, Vivek Venugopal, supervising the construction, the project got completed fast. That was how Sanjeevanam was opened in Kerala. Unlike all other Ayurveda hospitals, Sanjeevanam has an Ethics Committee, with the eminent neurosurgeon Dr K. Girish and Dr R.L. Saritha, former director of health department, Kerala, as members. There is a research department in Sanjeevanam. The ointment Reju Nuron, marketed by Fourrts company, used for curing diabetic wounds faster and for relief from neuropathic pain, was developed in the research department of Sanjeevanam. Dr Vijay Viswanathan, owner of M.V. Diabetics, Chennai, has been using this medicine on his patients for long and has certified to its effectiveness in treatment of diabetic wounds. He has also completed a research paper on it.

Rajan had prepared a chart for self-assessment. This was a revelation for me. He advised me that such self-examination is necessary for giving a new identity and to form to one's own personality. We all play multiple roles: as a son, husband, brother, colleague, neighbour or employee. A self-assessment will reveal the strength as well as the weakness of our personality and efforts can be made to make amends and make our life better. By going deeper into that analysis of the self, we will be able to realize desires that had been unfulfilled for long and bring out skills that had been dormant in us. If certain matters had been left out due to the pressing commitments of life, we can rectify that too. By employing this self-assessment method suggested by Rajan into practice, I was able to master the ever-evolving technical skills and stand tall at all times. Some shortfalls

in disposition and harshness in behaviour were polished
through this process. One of the instructions given in that
chart for self-betterment was to read books which I did
when the world came to be in the grips of corona virus.
I was able to choose the best books and bring back the
habit of reading, which had been neglected for long. A
book is my constant companion in all my travels.

Rajan, born in the Brahminical clan, was a pure
vegetarian. He had very few vices.

When he had to confine himself to the house due to
ailments connected with diabetes, we talked more on
the phone. One day, he complained that the *aaranmula
kannadi*, a mirror made of a special alloy of copper and
tin at Aaranmula in Kerala, which I had given him, had
been broken. He seemed to be very upset about it. He had
kept it in the puja room at home. As it is not made of glass,
the chances of it getting damaged are rare. Still, it broke.
He had wanted to see it as *kani* for Vishu.* On this day,
auspicious things are kept ready to be seen first in the
morning. He shared with me the apprehension that he may
not be able to see the kani for this Vishu. I comforted him
and sent another aaranmula kannadi. He called me happily
when it reached him. He informed me that he was feeling
better and that the doctor had said that he may relax some
of the restrictions. Now that there was no strict regimen to
be followed, he wanted to meet me and asked me to take a
flight to Bombay immediately.

I asked him for a week's time. He complained that it
was too long a time. We continued to talk and laugh for a

---

* Vishu is the harvest festival in Kerala falling on the first day of
Medam, the nineth month of the Malayalam calendar, usually in
the middle of April. 'Kani' means what one sees first on waking up.

long time. Then I had to cut the call to go to the washroom. Soon enough, Rajan called me back. As I took the call, I realized that it was Rajan's son Sreeram, Bombay High Court judge. 'My father is no more,' he said. I was almost paralysed with shock. It took me some time to process that the man who had been talking to me minutes ago was now no more. His apprehension that he may not be able to see the Vishu kani had come true.

8

Tradition of Preceptors
and the Film *Yugapurushan*

I believe that there is a bond that goes beyond many generations between Sree Narayana Gurudevan and me. Guru has been in my heart ever since I can remember. He continues to remain a source of strength and hope. My ancestors had the good fortune to enjoy the wisdom that emanated from Guru. Brahmasree Cholayil Maami Vaidyar, known as the present-day Dhanwanthari, was a member of my mother's family. Guru spoke thus about his skill in treatment.

> *immiyil araatha samghyayilla*
> *Maamiaal araatha rogamilla*
> (There is no amount that cannot be contained in the expression 'a little', *immi*
> There is no ailment that cannot be cured by Maami.)

My grandfather, Dr V.K. Padmanabhan, who too belonged to the Cholayil family had the good fortune to offer treatment to Guru.

When Guru was about to give up his bodily existence, he suffered from dysuria. When the discomfort due to

the ailment increased, my grandfather, who was working
in Ernakulam General Hospital at that time, visited
Gurudevan at Aluva Adwaithasramam and offered
treatment. He also considered it a blessing and had the
opportunity to travel with Guru by boat from Ernakulam
to Varkala. How can I, born in that family, do less than
enshrine Guru in my heart?

The relationship that my paternal grandfather, A.C.
Govindan, had with Guru was on a different level altogether.
When Guru visited our ancestral house, Arayamparambi at
Kodungaloor, A.C. Govindan, a small child then, had the
fortune to sit in Guru's lap. He has written a book titled
Children's Sree Narayana Guru. This is not the only source
from which I have imbibed the effulgence of Guru.

I have been tremendously influenced by the social
revolution that Sree Narayana Guru brought about in
our state. The consecration at Aruvippuram in 1888 and
the resultant bloodless reformation, his adage 'One caste,
one religion and one God for man', and proclamation that
'Man should behave well, whatever religion he belongs to',
attracted me a great deal. Sree Narayana Guru took up the
cause of promoting education for all, improving industries
and business, eradicating superstitions and outdated
customs, and called upon people to live in unity, keeping
truth and cleanliness. It is no wonder that he is seen as a
Viswa Guru, a Universal Preceptor.

When A.C. Govindan was a magistrate, there was a
dispute between the weavers and the Ezhavas, which led
to litigation. Guru reached Kozhikode to settle this issue.
At that time, A.C. Govindan stood with the weavers.
There are some verified stories about how the leaders of
the Ezhavas alienated Govindan for this and expelled him
from the community

I treasured a dream of making a film on Sree Narayana Guru's life to spread his teachings in society, when I was able to make enough money for it from my own efforts. Now I was in a position to fulfill that dream, and I decided to make the film. The name given to that film was *Yugapurushan*. A company named AVA Productions was registered for this purpose. There were no other thoughts in my mind except that my long-cherished dream was about to be realized. I had absolutely no experience in producing a film.

R. Sukumaran, a well-known painter and director, was ready to direct my film. He had done a lot of research on the philosophy enunciated by Guru. He was behind the success of films such as *Padamudra* and *Rajashilpi*. Our first priority was to find an actor who could enact the role of Guru. Only one endowed with extraordinary talent would be able to do this successfully. Our first choice was mega star Mammootty. He, too, was ready to do the role. But as the work was going on, he expressed his doubt whether he would be able to do justice to Gurudevan. His main concern was about keeping the calmness and serenity of Gurudevan's eyes throughout the project. He expressed his willingness to be a part of this film by taking up any other role.

The search for the hero was on. We wanted a man with the beautiful physique, size and brilliance that were the hallmark of Guru's personality. That search led us to the Tamil actor Thalaivasal Vijay. He used to act as a villain in Tamil films. When we saw his photographs, we felt that there was a resemblance to Guru's physical appearance. So we approached him.

He had never heard of Sree Narayana Guru. But he decided to assimilate the God-like character into himself.

For that he adopted his own methods. He changed some of his habits. He gave up all bad habits. He became a vegetarian and started practising meditation. As this regimen continued, his face radiated calmness and his eyes shone with compassion and commanding power. To maximize the effect, some sartorial changes were also introduced. This was done under the supervision of the famous make-up artist Pattanam Rasheed. He used prosthetic make-up, which was a very rare, high-quality and expensive product supplied from Bombay. Three to four hours had to be spent every day to put this make-up on the actor.

Guru had a uniquely structured body. To get this right in the character, a certain type of make-up was essential. To get Guru's facial features—his nose, ears and eyes—exactly in the actor, we made a mould of the head of the actor and attached these features on it. This method was used to get an accurate complexion of the body too. The director, Sukumaran, was an accomplished painter. He used that skill also in achieving perfection in the appearance of the hero. Such dedicated work brought four state awards for the film, including the one for the best make-up man.

Getting a location similar to Aruvippuram also proved to be difficult. The team had visited many places and was coming back without success. On the way back from Karnataka, the team reached the area near the Pazhassi Dam. There, they met an old man on the wayside. The director felt that he may be able to direct to the type of place they wanted. They stopped the vehicle and asked the old man about it. That venerable gentleman said that there was such a place nearby and pointed out the direction, even adding that we may be able to see it if we went there immediately. As per his direction, we went a short distance off the main road and found the place most suited for the shooting.

The place had the spiritual and natural qualities present at Aruvippuram. There was an *ammachi plavu* (jackfruit tree) and the surroundings of the place were exactly like those in Aruvippuram. Those who saw the film would not have thought that it was not shot at Aruvippuram.

The team decided to make it the location for the shooting and came back to the place where they had seen the old man. They wanted to thank him, but he was nowhere to be seen. Moreover, no one in that area had seen such a man. That meeting seemed to be an omen for better things to come.

At Kannur, we were able to find a hill that had the spiritual glow and natural beauty of Sivagiri. When the set of Sivagiri was made and the lamp was lit to commence shooting, many people gathered to pray.

The film could boast a long line of star actors. Mammootty, Siddique, Babu Antony, Navya Nair, Kalpana, Saikumar, Jagathi, Nandu and Kalabhavan Mani were among them.

Even before the puja and the starting of the shooting, news about *Yugapurushan* appeared in mainstream newspapers, other publications and television channels. It came to be discussed widely. It seemed that the Malayalam cinema world was waiting for such a film. We were all very happy about it.

There was an almost incessant flow of messages congratulating me on my efforts to make a film on the entire life of Sree Narayana Guru. They ranged from political and religious leaders, priests, superstars, others in the film world, friends, relatives, the holy ascetics of Sivagiri, including Sachidananda Swami, Vellappally Natesan, members of the Sree Narayana Dharma Paripalana Yogam and many others. Those who knew me and those who did not, came forward to felicitate me on my attempt. I too felt proud of myself for having taken up such an august project. I do not think there was another occasion when I felt so elated. A.V. Anoop, the producer, had become famous even before the film was released.

A special show was arranged at the studio in Thiruvananthapuram once the shooting was over to garner opinions and make an evaluation of the film before it was released. A gathering of eminent personalities, including Chief Minister V.S. Achuthanandan, came for the show. The chief minister watched the whole film, spending two hours and thirty-three minutes for the same. According to those who had accompanied the chief minister, this was a very rare occurrence. He responded openly to the media that was waiting to know his opinion. In his characteristic style, he raised his hands held together above his head and declared, 'I saw Guru.' He repeated the statement many times.

The media flashed news of the positive reviews given by those who saw it, including the chief minister. It was our creation. It was the child born of my heart. The news was discussed wherever Malayalees lived. A statement made by the Archbishop of Thiruvananthapuram exhorted everybody to see it.

Even more encouraging were the advice and instructions from Vellappally Natesan, general secretary of SNDP Yogam. He suggested that, through this film, a social revolution was being initiated in Kerala.

The secretary informed us that instructions had been issued to all branches of the Yogam asking the members to see the film. He warned us that a very large number of people, dressed in yellow, may arrive at the theaters even in lorries, and instructed us to make special arrangements for controlling the crowd.

This instruction came just days before the release of the film. We hastily found special security men to control the crowd and welcome the VIPs. There was no history of another film being released with such arrangements in Kerala. In Tamil Nadu, a film may be released at 2 a.m. to control the crowd. But nothing like that happens in Kerala. As the day of the release approached, my heart started throbbing faster in anticipation.

I was given a grand reception at Bengaluru for making the film.

Malayala Manorama, the Malayalam daily, devoted a whole page with pictures and articles on *Yugapurushan*.

Friday, 5 February 2010.

Yugapurushan was to be released on that day.

All those who had worked on the film assembled at a theatre in Ernakulam to see the first show.

My heart was beating faster and faster . . .

Shockingly, no one was queuing to see the movie.

The arches erected to welcome the viewers and the security guards employed to control the crowd remained still and unmoving.

There was no audience for the show.

Inquiries were made about the situation in other theaters.

It was the same. Some had even cancelled the show.

We stood looking at each other in silence, unable to comprehend what had happened. Our dejection was beyond description. We tried our best to keep the film running in theatres for at least a few days; all to no avail.

We had no idea about what had happened.

Like a nightmare, it was over.

Still, I remember, with gratitude, many who revered Guru, trying to woo people to the theaters.

By now lakhs of people have seen this film. Not in theatres. The majority of those who saw it on the Internet have marked it 'Excellent' in the column provided for evaluation. Even now, as I write this, someone in some corner of the world may be watching this film with a critical eye and ear. What does that indicate if not victory?

After the release of *Yugapurushan*, the institutions under the Sree Narayana movement and other social organizations noticed me. The recognition it brought me was tremendous. I was able to be a part of the establishment of the first medical college bearing Guru's name. I was also instrumental in establishing a chair in the name of Guru at Mumbai University.

Yugapurushan paved the way to my work as the chairman of the Patron Committee of the Confederation of Global Sree Narayana Organization, as the president of the Sree Narayana Institute of Medical Sciences, mentioned earlier, and as the adviser to the Sree Narayana Dharma Sangham at Sivagiri.

9

A Time of Love and Floods

The first film that was released under the banner of AVA Productions (AVA is the shortened form of Arayamparambil Vasavan Anoop, my full name) was *Pranayakaalam* (Time of Love). Work on the film based on the life of Narayana Guru had started, but I knew that it would take at least two years to complete. So when a new film opportunity presented itself, I decided to go ahead with it as it would give me an insight into the intricacies of helming a major film.

The film, directed by a newcomer, Uday Ananthan, was released in 2007. My first director! It won two state awards, giving me tremendous encouragement and the feeling that film production was also something I could handle. It also prompted me to involve myself more in the world of cinema.

The next production was a documentary titled *Before the Brush Dropped*. This was based on the life of the famous painter Raja Ravi Varma. It was directed by Vinod Mankara. This film brought the otherwise neglected field of painting into the limelight and placed it on the firm base of our culture. This film won a state award. But more than the award, it was the rare sense of acceptability that I gained that still warms my heart. The Kilimanoor Palace, in Thiruvananthapuram district, where Raja Ravi Varma was born, felicitated Vinod Mankara and me. Descendants of artist Thampuran conducted this function in the room where the great painter used to work, which is generally not open to the public. The rapture that I felt upon experiencing the unseen presence of Raja Ravi Varma, acclaimed as the Father of Indian Painting, is beyond description.

Cinema has blessed me with many memorable milestones. Sivagiri Mutt once arranged a reception for me, Sri R. Sukumaran, the director of the film *Yugapurushan*, and Thalaivasal Vijay, who acted in the role of Narayana Guru in that film. In the presence of all the revered ascetics of the Madom, in front of the consecration of Sarada Devi, Prakashananda Swami awarded me with the Sarada Award. Usually, the Madom does not hold such meetings for a film, but it was specially done for my film.

When my film won a place in the Guinness Book of World Records in 2018, the Cinema Producers' Association, Distributors' Association and FEFKA (Film Employees Federation of Kerala), the association of all the technical workers, felicitated me. This is a recognition granted by the film world. In 2018, my film *Viswaguru*, based on the life of Sree Narayana Guru, directed by Vijesh Mani, won the unique honour for being completed in fifty-one hours. Everything, from finding the artists, doing the make-up to getting the certificate from the Censor Board and releasing the film to the public, was completed in fifty-one hours.

I also wished to achieve a world record for soap making, i.e. a record of making the maximum number of soaps made by hand. But one of the stipulations of the authorities of the Guinness World Record prevented me from achieving it. They found that what the workers of Medimix company had achieved in fifty years will never be equalled or bettered by anyone else. For their records, they will consider only achievements that can be surpassed in the future. I feel blessed to have achieved what I desired, even though in a different field.

Such a contradiction happened to me while receiving the Golden Visa. This visa is considered as an honour accorded by the Dubai government to eminent persons who have proved their merit in different fields. You have to submit a detailed account of your work when applying for this visa. I submitted all the details, including my business and presence in the UAE. I hoped to be given the Golden Visa in the business segment. Instead, I was allotted the Golden Visa for artists. When they went through the details of my life, they were more impressed by my work and contribution in the field of drama and cinema. This view taken by the UAE government impressed on me the important revelation that artists, whatever their area of activity and the language they use, are respected universally. Thus, I became the proud possessor of the Golden Visa. It's indeed a certificate of honour for the contributions I have made in the world of arts for more than forty years.

I place utmost value to the recognition I received for making the documentary *Yaanam*, focusing on the achievements made by India in space research. The matter for the documentary was based on the chapter on Mangalyaan Mission in the work *My Odyssey: Memoirs of the Man behind the Mangalyaan Mission* by Dr Radhakrishnan, former chairman of ISRO.

Yaanam gave me more satisfaction and fame than many of my other films for which I had to spend crores. It's also the first science documentary film made in Sanskrit.

The reception that Vinod Mankara and I got for the making of this film was unparalleled. We were honoured

at the ISRO headquarters at Bengaluru in the presence
of more than 200 eminent scientists of our country. Dr S.
Somanath, the chairman of ISRO, felicitated us.

When I was a school student, I had just heard words
like 'outer space', 'scientist' and 'missile'. The places where
the missiles were made were under strict surveillance and
security. It was at this place that we had been invited to
receive felicitations. What a unique and unforgettable
experience! We were also felicitated at the Indian Institute
of Astrophysics under the leadership of the director
Dr Annapurni Subramaniam.

We gained immense goodwill through the making of this
documentary. There were certain factors that made *Yanam*
popular among the people. A question about this film was
included in the popular quiz programme, *Kaun Banega
Crorepati?* hosted by the acclaimed film star Amitabh
Bachchan. The question, pertaining to which language this
film was made in, helped in spreading awareness about
this film. After this, some of the Malayalam channels also
included questions on this film in their quiz programmes
which also added to the popularity of *Yanam*.

My family was blessed with another rare honour when
we were invited to Sriharikota, Andhra Pradesh, to witness
the launch of Chandrayaan-3—an event that had caught
the attention of the whole world.

Cinema has bestowed me many national and local
awards. This triumphal march started with my first film.
The short film in Tamil, *Appuvin Nayakan* (2008), was
directed by Santosh Sethumadhavan, son of the legendary
director Sethumadhavan. The story stressed on the values
of life and the relationship among the members of a family.
This film won the National Film Award for the 'Best Film
for Family Values'.

As I mentioned earlier, my life story also includes an incident when a rehearsal camp for a play led to the birth of a film. Often those who are involved in plays and films visit rehearsal camps as they are useful in gathering diverse opinions and evaluating the efforts we make in our plays. Once, director Ranjith visited my rehearsal camp and expressed an opinion. He wanted me to conduct a workshop for the actors in the plays to be trained for acting in films. He felt a novel area in acting and sensibility could be generated through this. I realized the significance of such a training camp and agreed to do it. We invited participants and received more than 800 applicants, out of which thirty-two were shortlisted. Those who completed the training successfully could potentially be a part of ensuing films.

We needed some interesting material to be used for the training. It had to be different from the usual lot, with characters and scenes that the audience had not seen before, full of dramatic situations; a script that kept the tempo of interest alive and continued to hold the attention of the viewers till the very end. The organizers started searching for such kind of material. In the end, it was Ranjith himself who came up with a suggestion of using a novel that had been published as a serial in the *Mathrubhumi Weekly*, *Paaleri Manikyam Oru Paathiraa Kolapaathakathinte Katha*, written by T.P. Rajeevan. It had been published as a novel by then. So I bought the book and started reading it.

During the shooting for *Yugapurushan*, Mammootty once asked me, 'How is your reading of *Paleri Manikyam* going on?' I stood thinking how he had come to know about my interest in the book. He continued, 'If you have any plans to make a film with it, I am ready to act in it.' I went ahead and deputed Ranjith to direct the film, which went on to become one of the most extraordinary films ever made in Malayalam. Mammootty revealed his histrionic acumen by taking up three roles in it. He won the Kerala State Award for the 'Best Actor'. The 'Best Actress Award' went to Shweta Menon for her role in the same film. I received the award for the 'Best Film'. In that film, we were able to include all of the thirty-two people who had participated in the training programme.

The first film I acted in is *Kadaksham* (2010). Suresh Gopi was in the lead role. This film directed by Adv. Sasi Paravoor won the Kerala State Award for the 'Best Story' for the year 2010. The next year, I made *Christian Brothers* with Mohanlal as the hero and directed by Joshy. *Aaru Sundarimaarude Katha,* which was produced in 2012, found a place in the *Limca Book of World Records* for introducing 'Finger Dance' in a film. This film was directed by Rajesh K. Abraham.

In 2014, I made a film on the story of four girls born together and bearing a close resemblance to one another titled *Enna Satham Indha Neram* in Tamil. The girls who acted in the film were also quadruplets: Athidhi, Aakruthi, Akshithi and Aapthi. Guru Ramesh directed the film. This film also found a place in the *Limca Book of World Records* for featuring four girls with a close resemblance to each another.

I am not going to mention all the films I produced or acted in. Here, I have mentioned only the special ones. Great cinema is a result of great team work. Success and recognition will come when each one does their part with care and perfection. I feel gratified in that matter. I value all the awards and the recognition I have gained from this.

There are a few more awards that I must mention here. *Guppy*, directed by the newcomer John Paul, won five state awards. *Ishq*, which was shortlisted for Best Film at the National Awards, was screened as the inaugural film at the Goa International Film Festival. It won the National Award for cinematography. *Oolu* was selected in the Indian Panorama section for the Cannes Short Film Festival. Another film that is worthy of mention is *Chaaya*.

I acted as the lead role in Sohanlal's *Appuvinte Sathyanweshanam*. It was a 'Gandhian' character. This film won four international awards.

Furthermore, I derived immense joy and satisfaction from the documentary titled *Greenman*, which amassed much national and international acclaim. This was based on the life of environmentalist Kaloor Balan. Directed by V.K. Subhash, the film is a warning against global warming.

In a span of sixteen years, I acted in thirteen films in Malayalam, Tamil and English (Hollywood). I appeared in twelve serials also at a time when we had only Doordarshan, Asianet and Surya television channels. The most recent film I acted in is *Achanoru Vazha Vechu*. I will act in more films if I get meaty roles, where I can showcase my ability to act.

Some Film Stars and My Experiences with Them

We will never forget the tsunami that lashed the coastal areas of Kerala and Tamil Nadu on 26 December 2004. It created havoc. The World Malayalee Council was active in offering help to the victims. Velankanni and Kanyakumari in Tamil Nadu, Alappad and Vallikavu in Kollam district, and Cherai in Ernakulam district in Kerala were the worst affected. In turn, we selected Vallikavu to conduct our relief operations. There were hundreds of fisher folk who had been the victims of the lashing waters. The World Malayalee Council, under Priyadas Mangalath, built a community hall for them there.

Our presence and support gave a lot of hope and happiness to the people of that area. We were implementing schemes to help those affected to come back to a life of normalcy. When the construction of the community hall was completed, we thought of having a film star at the inaugural ceremony. I was entrusted with the task of finding one and accepted the responsibility with joy. The locals were excited at the prospect of seeing a star they had only seen on the silver screen. I found an actor whom I knew from my college days, and he agreed to come for the function. I called him the day before the inauguration to remind him of the event. Then he placed a most unexpected condition before me: He wanted Rs 1 lakh for the inauguration. I felt revolted by the inhuman demand. It was a welfare programme for which many people had contributed out of humane considerations. This artist too should have come with a helping hand instead of demanding payment for himself. Instead, he had appeared as the personification of self-interest and cruelty and stated his usual rate for an appearance. The organizers were in a tough spot. The council could easily raise that amount demanded by the star. But all the members involved in it were of the opinion that a payment like this should not be made for a humanitarian work. So, I started thinking of finding another actor who would be ready to come for the inauguration gratis. It was difficult to get a well-known actor in such a short time. My colleagues entrusted me with that responsibility again. With a disturbed mind, I tried calling many people. Many were ready to come, but they were not free on the day of the function. Many of those who were close to me were at shooting sites far away. One of the people I called was actor Jayaram. I explained the situation to him and requested him to suggest somebody else if he was not free. He listened to me carefully and ended the conversation with a promise that he would do his best.

My mind was in turmoil. I was waiting for a call that would bring a solution to the problem. The call came that evening. It was Dileep, a renowned actor. After an exchange of pleasantries, he said, '*Jayaramettan* [Actor Jayaram] had talked to me. I am at Ernakulam now. You can send someone here with a car.' His words were like a shower of comforting, cool drops of water on our parched hearts. Dileep enjoyed more popularity and recognition than the actor we had first approached. So we were sure that this substitute would be even more warmly welcomed by the people of this village. Dileep reached on time and inaugurated the community hall. That remains an unforgettable incident in my own life and in that of the villagers there.

There is another incident connected with the tsunami that still sends shivers down my spine. On 25 December that year, I was at the Cherai beach with my family for Christmas celebrations. We had planned to fly to Sri Lanka early in the morning. Usually on vacation trips like this, I book hotels on the sea coast. But this year, I had made a change from the usual practice and booked rooms in one of the hill stations in Sri Lanka. That saved our lives.

As we landed in Sri Lanka and were on our way to our hotel, we could see water gushing onto the road. It was with great difficulty that we reached our destination. By that time, the tsunami had started its reign of destruction.

All means of communication were disrupted. As the phones went dead, all connection with the outside world was cut. We were worried about how to get back. I was the global general secretary of the World Malayalee Council at that time. When I could not be contacted on phone, those who tried to get me were worried. This continued till the telephone connections were restored. At Cherai too, the waves lashed the beach and caused much destruction immediately after we had left the place. At both places, we had escaped by the breadth of a hair, as the saying goes.

I first met Mammootty, the superstar of Malayalam film industry, when I went to his house to invite him for an important meeting of the Malayalee Club. He did not respond positively to that invitation. But soon, something happened which increased my respect for him.

This happened after the success of the Malayalee Meet organized by the Federation of All India Marunadan Malayalee Association (FAIMA). My work as one of the main organizers of that meeting had caught the attention of many. I was invited to the first meeting to plan a show that Kairali TV was to hold in Delhi. It was their strong impression of me that prompted them to invite me for a meeting of many eminent personalities. Serious discussions were held for making it a grand success under the leadership of Rajagopal, former Union Minister of State, P.C. Alexander, former Governor, and Mammootty. Many of those who participated in the discussion mentioned my name many times. This made Alexander ask who Anoop was. Before I could get up, Mammootty stood up saying, 'I will introduce him. Anoop is a young industrialist, doing a lot of good work for the Malayalees living outside the state. He runs Medimix company and is involved in philanthropic activities too. But the one thing that makes him really great is that he is a committed artist too.' I had not expected such words and felt touched by his speech.

Compared to the stalwarts assembled there, I was just a newcomer and there was no need for Mammootty to make such a detailed introduction of a young man. On that day, I learnt the lesson that all our selfless work and actions based on strong values will bring recognition even at the most unexpected moments.

'I am coming to Chennai. Can I see you when I am there?' This was a call from Alappuzha, a municipality in Kerala. It was Fahadh Faasil, son of the eminent director Fazil and an actor himself. I told him that he could see me on any day except Saturday. A felicitation meeting was arranged for me in Chennai after I had won a place in the Guinness Book of World Records. As I had to take part in that meeting, I would not be free on Saturday. On hearing about the meeting, Fahadh asked whether he could also attend the meeting. It was a sincere question and I was surprised to hear it. Usually, the organizers have to approach eminent people to request them to attend meetings. But in my case, it was just the opposite. I welcomed him with utmost joy. He came to Chennai at his own expense. He visited my house and office as if we had been acquainted for a long time. He asked questions with a childlike curiosity and came for the felicitation meeting as a distinguished guest and gave a speech. In that, he spoke about how impressed he had been by the workings of the Medimix company, about the orderly functioning and neatness he saw there, and the exemplary behaviour of the employees. He wanted others to follow this style. Later he told his wife Nazriya on the phone that if he had known me and seen all this earlier, his behaviour would have been different.

The general feeling is that the new generation of film actors, who have achieved success in the field, are all very proud and do not show any respect towards their elders.

Fahadh's visit taught me how personal experience can correct many preconceived notions.

Let me now speak about an incident that happened while I was travelling by plane. I was going to Delhi to serve as the chief guest at a function and present a skit.

The passenger seated next to me seemed familiar. As he had worn a mask, I could not see his face clearly. A person shorter than me, with an unshaven face. Then suddenly, I realized who he was. It was Rajinikanth, the actor whom lakhs of people worshiped for his acting acumen. I also realized that no one else in the plane could tell who he was. Since his official name was different, even the staff of the airlines had not recognized him. If others got to know his identity, they would quickly gather around him. I, too, long cherished the dream of meeting Rajinikanth in person and having a photo taken with him. Now that rare chance had presented itself. I introduced myself and shook hands with him. As we were talking, I expressed my desire to have a selfie taken with him. He agreed and removed the mask only after making sure that no one was watching. We continued to talk till the end of the journey. As we landed, I was surprised to see him take his own luggage. He had been travelling without even an assistant. When those with little stardom threw huge tantrums, here was the 'Thalaivar', the idol of millions of theatre goers, humbly collecting and carrying his own luggage. When I offered to help in taking the luggage from the overhead compartment, he politely refused. He told me that this was the way he always travelled. Like any other passenger, he walked out with his bag. There was no crowd waiting to see him. But there was another crowd, specially summoned to welcome a spiritual leader who had also arrived by another plane!

During the flight, we talked about plays and films. When I told him that I was going to Delhi to present a skit, he looked surprised. He had heard about Medimix and me before. He had thought that I was just a businessman. When I told him about my involvement in the world of plays and films and the recognition I had gained in both the fields, there was an added warmth in our conversation. As we shook hands on parting ways, I felt sure of the additional ardour above our coincidental meeting. 'Call me if you need anything,' were the final words he uttered before we parted. I took it as just a word of courtesy to someone he had met accidentally. For me, his willingness to pose for a selfie with me and the chance I had got to talk with him were evidence of his good manners.

But to my utter surprise, there was a sequel to this meeting. Rajinikanth's manager called me on the phone. 'Rajini sir has asked that I convey something that he forgot to mention during the flight.' I was anxious to know what it was. He told me that Rajinikanth and his family had been using Medimix soap for many years. Such a revelation coming from someone like Rajinikanth created a wave of thrill in our Medimix family.

There are scenes of the heroine Jayasudha, selling Medimix soap in the film *Apoorva Raagangal,* directed by the famous director Kailasam Balachandar. This film had gained popularity among the audience all over the world. That was also the first film in which Rajinikanth acted. The film played a crucial role in making Medimix soap popular and accepted by consumers. When the film was remade in Hindi, the director insisted on using only Medimix soap in those scenes!

Our Delhi trip had another social significance. I posted the photo I had taken with him on Facebook. There were rumours that Rajinikanth was planning to enter politics and would be going to Delhi for that. With my post, his journey to Delhi was confirmed and innumerable guesses were made on it. Many people, including those from the media, approached me. When this photo appeared on some TV channels, there were also requests for an interview with me. If I got so much of attention just for a chance to travel with him, I can't imagine how much respect the people and the media have for Rajinikanth.

In another instance, I was able to know the simple nature, magnanimity and love that the Rajni family exhibits. This happened during a wedding in Kochi. The bridegroom was from Chennai. I recognized one lady who had come with the bridegroom's party. It was Latha, Rajinikanth's wife. I approached her and introduced myself. She asked me, 'You live in Chennai; but why haven't you come to our house? You must come,' she invited me. The warmth and sincerity in her words surprised me.

I have known Mohanlal for several decades. He was my senior at M.G. College, Thiruvananthapuram. His individuality has left me surprised many a time. Our relationship became stronger with the association we had with the Malayalee Club. Mohanlal regularly played shuttle badminton there. The film *Bharatham*, in which he acted as the hero, was shot at this club. This led to more meetings for our friendship to strengthen. Soon our families became friends.

Once, a few of us who were actively involved in presenting dramas, were seated in a corner of the Malayalee Club, speaking, at length, about a rehearsal camp. The camp for a new play usually started with a puja ceremony. The script was to be handed over at that time. Moreover, the rehearsal camp was to be held at Dr Sidhan's house. We were discussing this camp when Mohanlal came over. 'What are you all planning here?' he asked in his characteristic style. First, we were a bit hesitant, but then we told him about our discussion. He seemed really interested and asked for some details, which I gave him. Before leaving, he asked for the address of the place where the puja was to be held.

It was the day of the puja. We were getting ready for the ceremony. Suddenly, the lady who was to act in the leading role ran in and announced something, her eyes filled with wonder. We realized she had seen Mohanlal walk in through the gate. His visit had created a lot of enthusiasm and encouragement in the camp. Here was a star who mesmerized the audience on the silver screen but also loved less interesting arenas of entertainment.

Lal always respected and accepted the bonds of friendship. Let me share an incident that evinced this. A group of badminton players in the Malayalee Club decided to hold a tournament. All of the members were expected to take part in the tournament. Mohanlal was a bit hesitant. 'Please exempt me from playing in the tournament. If I play and lose, it will be flashed across the news. But I am ready to do any work that you ask me to do.'

We accepted this plea and asked him, 'Are you ready to be a line umpire?' He readily agreed and did the work assigned to him with great enthusiasm throughout the tournament.

As we were family friends, we used to holiday together. I remember one incident when his son Pranav was a small boy. Lal's wife, Suchitra, is the daughter of the famous film producer Balaji. He had a farmhouse far away from the city of Chennai. Once, it was decided that we would meet there for our get-together that weekend. It is not easy for one who is not very sure of the route to find this place.

Mobile phones had not made their appearance yet, so it was quite possible to get lost.

It was not possible to make inquiries along the deserted route. When Lal invited us to the farm, I told him of this difficulty.

'Don't worry. There is a milestone at the point where the path to the farmhouse begins. I will ask somebody to stand there to direct you,' he said.

'We will be coming in a Fiat car. I will be driving. You can tell the person this so that he will be able to identify us,' I told Lal, and he agreed to do so.

We were on our way on the appointed day. Within an hour, we had left the city limits. We were nearing the spot Lal had mentioned. I was searching for our guide. If I went ahead without meeting this man, the whole journey would be in vain. I had to be sure of the place where we had to turn to the side road. Then in the distance, I could see someone sitting on the milestone that Lal had mentioned. As I stopped the car in front of that figure, my wife and I were shocked. It was Mohanlal himself! We had not dreamt of such a celebrated film star waiting for us on the road.

In the days when the world was affected by the corona virus, many artists in the field of drama and cinema also suffered a great deal. Many lost their livelihood. Mohanlal came forward to comfort those who were in the grip of anxiety and offered help. He called all of them, from the light boy onwards, personally, and made inquiries. He called me too and discussed this unexpected calamity.

Before I conclude this chapter on my association with those in the field of cinema, there are a few more names that remain fresh in my memory. They are Mukesh R. Mehta and Varnachithra Subair, who were with me in a number of good films.

10

Centenary of the Malayalee Club and My Organizational Ventures

The Malayalee Club, Chennai, has played a major role in developing my power of organization and artistic talents.

The Club was born from the oldest association of Malayalees in the world. It was established in 1897. The Golden Jubilee of India's independence and the centenary of the club were celebrated almost at the same time (1996–97). The celebrations were planned for a year. I was the Secretary at that time. In the Club's history, many stalwarts have achieved glory.

I was a member of the executive committee of the Club for more than twelve years. When I first came to Chennai, I started going to the Club to play shuttle badminton and realized the Club held drama and rehearsals sessions. This excited the actor in me.

It was through the Malayalee Club that I gained the experience in organizational work, managing committees and larger groups, and developing leadership qualities. I had been a member of the committee since 1986. The ability and strength that I gained through those ten years helped me in carrying out my duties as the secretary at the time of the centenary celebrations. The programmes

I organized for the celebrations were novel and exciting for the Malayalees of Chennai. We conducted eighteen programmes in a year as part of the centenary celebrations.

When I first started getting involved in organizing programmes, I barely had the confidence to stand up and give a welcome address. The thought that I was insignificant in front of all the eminent personalities around me, held me back. Stage fright prevented me from expressing what I wanted to say. But my mind did not think of withdrawing in the face of these limitations. Instead, my mind went on prompting me to overcome all the shortcomings and move forward. The Malayalee Club provided me with the platform to sharpen my skills. I started making use of every opportunity that came my way and took care to act with utmost care. This slowly made people take notice of me. I realized the responsibilities we uphold help make society a vibrant and safe place to live. The power and the lessons that I learnt from that knowledge were immense. The power as well as the weakness of a people is greatly affected by the quality of leadership. This prompted me to accept greater responsibilities as a leader. The Malayalee Club was the arena that taught me all this. Many great leaders like T.G. Menon, (Gopiyettan for me), K.V. Nair, Smt Bharathi Raja, K. Vasudevan, and Ravindran (IPS) were present with support and encouragement. Friends such as Nandagovind, K.P.A. Latheef and G. Vijayakumar supported me at all times. Later, I relinquished my post with the satisfaction that I had completed all the duties assigned to me in an exemplary manner.

Many organizations that work hard with a laudable aim in view, fail when they start searching for power.

Minds that have not yet been rescued from egoism and false ideas of racial superiority play the villains here. Some fear the entry of others. But all such matters never touched our Club. There, the system was to accept diverse opinions and act on democratic principles. I considered only the ability of the individual in selecting members for the Club. I was quite aware of the power that we gain when people of diverse abilities come together. Caste, religion, financial position or high birth were irrelevant. Humanitarian activities adhering to these principles made the Club better and more popular.

The first programme in connection with the centenary celebrations was the Swathi Sangeetha Nritholsavam and the dedication of the Swathi Award. It was a desire to move away from the beaten path that led us to Swathi Thirunal Rama Varma. Chennai hosts many noteworthy music concerts every year. The media provides good coverage for all of them. But there was no Malayalee presence in those concerts. Music sabhas in Chennai did not consider the great composer Swathi Thirunal. A discussion regarding this lack of acceptance of his genius led to the suggestion of holding a music festival in the name of Swathi Thirunal and presenting an award in his name. This suggestion was made by my colleague, Kala Sasikumar, who was an expert on music also. We accepted the suggestion and the Swathi Festival was held with great pomp. The Swathi Sangeethotsavam and award presentation that is held every year now was started by the Kerala government on seeing the popularity that our effort attained. The first award given by the Club was to the vocalist Semmangudi Srinivasa Iyer. Later, it was awarded to Yesudas also. The first award committee consisted of the famous cine artist and dancer Shobhana, T.V. Gopalakrishnan and Gopika Varma.

The centenary celebrations were inaugurated on 18 August 1996 by T.N. Seshan, Chief Election Commissioner. The variety entertainment programme was opened by A.C. Shanmughadas, Health Minister of Kerala. There was a Bharatanatyam performance by Shobhana and Ganamela by Yesudas in October.

One programme item specifically chalked out for the centenary was a workshop on public speaking. Public speaking is 'the Act of Persuasion' according to Aristotle. The gifted speaker Chakiyar Rajan was the instructor. Some of the delightful insights that Rajan presented at the session remain ever fresh in my memory.

An example of one speaker who stole valuable time from the invited guests and ended his note without actually welcoming anybody, was a revelation. The Sanskrit words *mitham cha saaraamchiva chohi vagmitha* (a speech must be short and contain only important points) should always be borne in mind by all speakers.

I too have been the 'victim' of these type of events where guests are formally welcomed at a meeting. Once I was introduced as the 'one who sold products that harm the skin'. When he went on praising me for this, someone seated on the platform tried to correct him. Even then, the speaker reiterated his words: 'Yes, selling products that harm the skin.' What a slip of the tongue!

Just as Indira Gandhi is introduced as the daughter of Mahatma Gandhi, some people suggest that Anoop is as efficient as his father, Dr Sidhan. Here, my uncle became my father. One major lesson I learnt from the workshop was that one should never showcase how shallow one's knowledge is by speaking about things one is not sure of.

This training later made me take up public speaking as a passion and helped me speak without hesitation at many large gatherings. Now, when I talk to the new generation, I base my words on my own experience.

I am reminded of a joke that Rajan presented as a part of the training. An organization decided that a member must crack a joke at the beginning of each of its executive meetings. This was based on the assumption that such a start would reduce tension and make members more cheerful. This practice was successfully carried out for some time. At one particular meeting, one speaker delivered a funny story. Yet, not one member smiled, let alone laugh. He renewed his effort by explaining his joke thinking that they might not have understood it the first time. Still there was no response from the others. Feeling that there was something eerie about the situation, he glanced at the paper on which the agenda of the meeting was written. Then he realized that it was a meeting to condole the death of an important member—a most solemn occasion.

We find many who state things without understanding the context of the situation. In the beginning, I used to face the audience on the strength of the speech that I had on the paper with me. There would be only a few lines, and I would happily read them out. Slowly I found that I could present things well without the paper in hand. My stage fright disappeared. I feel that stage fright is a misnomer for what I felt while making speeches because even at that time, I was performing on stage as a hero without any difficulty.

As we have talked about the performance of the speaker who welcomes the gathering, we should not neglect to mention the one who is deputed to give the vote of thanks. There are many who make a lengthy speech when it can be restricted to two or three sentences. You can still hear

words like these: 'Let me thank Sri Kuttappayi, who made
the food for the delegates at this meeting, Sri Vinod, who cut
the drumsticks for it, Kittan Chettan who made the knife
and Sri Thankappan, who was kind enough to sharpen the
knife.' Unfortunately, such speeches will continue with the
customary welcome and vote of thanks.

I have never actively searched for ways to reach the
position of a leader. Mostly the mantle has fallen on me, as
if it were predestined. As I complete organizing each event,
as I fulfill each responsibility given to me, I learn something
new, and this learning still continues.

During the centenary celebrations of the Malayalee Club,
we held an array of events including a drama competition,
jugalbandi, food festival, sports and games as well as the
Golden Jubilee celebrations of India's independence and
the centenary of the birth of Subhas Chandra Bose and
V.K. Krishna Menon. These memorable programmes were
held under the leadership of K.V. Nair as convenor and
Gokulam Gopalan as chairman. The *Souvenir* published
next year in connection with this is a document of history
for the Malayalees of Chennai.

Dr Pavithran, Dr V.P. Sidhan and Dr P. Balakrishnan
are seen as the Trinity of Friends in the Malayalee Club
circles. In the souvenir published at the centenary, Dr P.
Balakrishnan has mentioned how theatre work started at
the club on the insistence of Dr Sidhan who was at that
time a senior student at the Medical College. All three of
the above-mentioned were students at the Kilpauk Medical
College, Chennai. Dr Sidhan and Dr P. Balakrishnan had
acted in plays together even in 1955. This play, named
Manashasthrathinte Makkaar, was penned by M.P. Sivadasa
Menon, who was already famous in the theatre circles
of Chennai.

Dr P. Balakrishnan has written about a young man who had come to Chennai seeking a chance to sing in films. Dr Balakrishnan first made him come to his house and heard him sing. Then, knowing that the young man was short of money, he got him chances to participate in various entertainment programmes. This boy, K.J. Yesudas, later became the emperor of playback singing. Dr P. Balakrishnan and Augustine Joseph, Yesudas's father, were friends. Balakrishnan made his friend's son take part in many programmes at the Malayalee Club. Dr P. Balakrishnan, who was one of the office-bearers of the club at that time, once mentioned in a *Souvenir* article, the need to search for vouchers for payment of Rs 50, Rs 60 and Rs 100, etc. to Yesudas.

Dr Pavithran, a writer and a journalist, had served as the member of the working committee of the Madras Regional Division of the Film Censor Board of India. The trio created a golden era for arts at the Malayalee Club. I became their successor and the youngest secretary in the history of the club. I served in that capacity for four years.

Another place where I rendered my services was the Asan Memorial Association. This was first formed with 100 Malayalees as members. A.K. Gopalan, who established this, should be remembered with gratitude by all the Malayalees in Chennai. The association lays stress on the development of the language and literature of Kerala. The Asan Memorial Poetry Award, which has gained respect and repute in cultural and artistic fields, is given by this association. This is the biggest award for poetry in Malayalam. When he came to know that I had left the position as an office-bearer of the Malayalee Club, A.K. Gopalan asked me to be actively involved in the association and work as an committee member. I was

already a member. The committee at that time had stalwarts
such as Prem Nazir, K.P. Ummer, K.S. Sethumadhavan,
M.O. Joseph and V. Abdulla serving in it. I was entering
such an august group. I feel it is pertinent to mention the
story of a strike connected with this association which runs
more than ten educational institutions.

The Asan Memorial School was functioning in a land
taken on lease from the Kerala government. The compound
lying next to it was used by the students as a playground.
But this was not a part of the leased land. All of a sudden,
the government took possession of this land and built
a wall around it. Now there was no playground for the
school. The land was quickly handed over to the tourism
department. The department gave it to the Kerala Tourism
Development Corporation (KTDC). The Malayalees of
Chennai saw this as a blow to their pride. They started
agitating against the action taken. I too became an
active participant in the protests, being a member of the
Malayalee associations. As the protest was at its peak, it
was rumoured that the government was planning to sell
it to a private company. My personal view was that the
land should be handed back to the school. The members
of the Kerala Samajam felt that if the land was sold to a
private company, it will result in a loss of prestige for the
members of the Malayalee associations there and started
proceedings to stall the sale. I was totally in support of that
move. Some people saw this as an indication that I was
going against the interests of the Asan group. In fact, there
was some truth in that. I did not want the loss of the land
to be seen as a result of the lack of initiative on the part
of the Malayalees. Most of the Malayalee organizations
agreed with that view. All of them wanted to have the land
kept for the use of the Malayalees. Due to the intensity

of the agitation and on the insistence of many including myself, Chief Minister Oommen Chandy took the decision not to sell the land. Though this decision gave some relief, a permanent solution took a long time. Later, the agitation was called off on the basis of an agreement that the Tourism Corporation would build a hotel at the land taken over by the government. Five rooms and a hall in that building would be given for the use of the Malayalee associations in Chennai. There was a clause that the rooms and the hall would be allotted only on the basis of an official request from Kerala Samajam, the CTMA and AIMA.* This dispute, which started when E.K. Nayanar was the chief minister, continued through the tenures of Chandy and V.S. Achuthanandan.

The demand that the land should be given back to the school was strongly upheld by A.K. Gopalan and others. It was at this time that Achuthanandan came to lay the foundation stone for the hotel. My name was included in the list of those who were participating in the function. It was felt that if I stood with the other side, the strength of the demand made by the Asan School would be lessened. So a group of well-wishers informed me that they would remove me from the Asan Memorial Committee. But when the agitation came to an end, my acceptance among all only became stronger. This became evident when I got a call from A.K. Gopalan. I went to meet him thinking that it would be to express his displeasure at my change of stance. But what he told me really surprised me. He asked me to be more involved with the activities of the Asan Memorial institutions. He wanted me to be the vice president of

* CTMA: Confederation of Tamilnadu Malayalee Associations; AIMA: All India Malayalee Association

the association and become the chairman of the College Managing Committee. I bow my head at this large-hearted gesture. On that disputed land stands the hotel Rain Drops run by KTDC. The office of NORKA (Non-resident Keralites Affairs) is situated there.

There is a coordinating committee for the more than 120 Malayalee organizations in Tamil Nadu—CTMA. The founder president was M.P. Purushothaman. C. Velayudhan, Abraham, chairman of Aban Group, K.V. Nair and V. Parameswaran were the other founder members. Thousands of Malayalees took part in the Onam celebrations held under the auspices of this association in 2001, named Aavanipoovarangu. I was the chairman of the association at that time. In 2001, Mammootty was the celebrity guest. Malayalees in Chennai wait for the day of Aavanipoovarangu to celebrate Onam. In fact, it is the CTMA that presents the Dr Sidhan Memorial Drama Award every year.

The Federation of All India Marunadan Malayalee Association (FAIMA) is another important Malayalee organization. The All India Malayalee Meet that FAIMA organized in Delhi in 1999 turned out to be an unforgettable event in my life. I was the convener of this meeting held at Pragati Maidan. The eminent people who were responsible for conducting that meeting gave me that onerous responsibility. I accepted that challenging job with immense joy.

Holding a meeting of that dimension in Delhi in those days was not an easy job. I had to be at the helm of affairs while staying in Chennai and meet many important people. For this, I had to visit Delhi many times. Later I stayed in Delhi to ensure that the meeting was a great success. Kerala House became the centre of activity for this. We got the support of the Kerala government for this meeting.

Prominent among those who stood with me to make the programme a success were Firoz, the information officer in the PR department, and the eminent journalist V.K. Madhavan Kutty. Even after many decades, Delhi has not witnessed such a grand meeting of Malayalees.

Five eminent Malayalees were to be honoured at that meeting. Four of them were selected unanimously, namely Gokulam Gopalan, V.P. Sidhan, M.A. Abraham and Ujjaala Ramachandran. The fifth person under consideration was Yusuff Ali. There was some difference of opinion in selecting him. At that time this name had not been prominently heard in any field. After further consideration, it was decided to honour him as an upcoming genius for whom such a recognition would be an encouragement. Time has proved how right we were in our assessment. Yusuff Ali has grown to be Malayalee's pride in the business field in the past two decades. In 2000, he opened his first mall.

I have had the good fortune to know the magnanimity and nobility of Yusuff Ali personally. Once an online meeting was organized by Minister P. Rajiv to discuss the problems related to doing business in Kerala. There were only twenty selected participants in it. On seeing my name in the list, Yusuff Ali spoke highly about me and Medimix products.

At that time, he mentioned that Medimix products were not available for him. I listened to his words with joy but neglected to send the products to him.

At another online meeting of the World Malayalee Council in which thousands of eminent people participated, he repeated the complaint that he had not received the Medimix products. This was a live programme. Isaac John Pattaniparambil, managing editor of *Khaleej Times* and a friend of mine, informed me about this. He reminded me of the hundreds of companies waiting for a chance to introduce their products to Yusuff Ali. Here he had personally made the request. This must be because of his confidence in Medimix products. Immediately, I made arrangements to provide our products for him at Abu Dhabi.

Yusuff Ali sent me a letter thanking me and expressing his happiness on receiving the products. I am still in awe of his humility and goodwill.

Once the ruler of Abu Dhabi had some skin problems. He spoke about it to Yusuff Ali, who is very close to the royal family. Immediately, Yusuff Ali sent him some Medimix soap to use. He had removed the cover so that the name would not be known. After a few days, the king spoke about the effect of using the soap and inquired about the name of the product. Then he told him that it was the Medimix soap and gave him another one with a wrapper. This is a private matter. But Yusuff Ali spoke about it at a media conference in Kerala in which I too was present. We have been keeping a good relationship from the time he started the Lulu Supermarkets and Lulu Hypermarkets. This has played a significant role in the rise of the demand for Medimix products in the international market.

The World Malayalee Council is an international association of Malayalees. I was responsible for establishing the Madras chapter of the council. Let me share a backstory that led to this. An acquaintance once called me to ask whether I could do something to help a man whose wife had died while they were travelling by train in Germany. He wanted to bring her body to India and wanted help in handling the legal formalities. I understood the helplessness of the man and decided to do something about it. I searched the Internet and found the phone number of the representative of the World Malayalee Council. I called him immediately and impressed on him the urgency of the matter. He took immediate steps to help the affected man. This made me feel that we should have this organization in Chennai also. In 2001, the Madras chapter was started under my leadership. Even to this day, it is the biggest association of Malayalees at the international level.

There is a glowing chapter in the work rendered by this council. This was the collection of consent letters from people at Mannathur village of Muvatupuzha in Kerala for donating their eyes after death. All the residents of the village gave their consent to do it. Three lakh nineteen thousand people from twenty-nine panchayats agreed to be a part of this campaign—a world record. The removal of the eye after death, without causing any disfigurement to the face, would result in the gift of eyesight for another person. When the World Malayalee Council took up this mission, a huge number of people supported it. At first, the villagers were reluctant, but the selfless work done by some eminent people made them change their mind. This included Minister T.M. Jacob, famous playback singer Yesudas, and eminent cine artists like Mohanlal and Kunchacko Boban. They came in person and explained the matter to the people. This induced a large number of villagers to agree to donate their eyes.

Mannathur became the venue for this work, as it was connected with a friend Nithyasathya. He was an inmate in the ashram of Guru Nitya Chaitanya Yati in Ooty. He had wanted to remain a bachelor and dedicate himself to the service of spreading the message of the Guru. But the Guru wanted to see Nithyasathya as a householder. Guru Nitya Chaitanya Yati spoke about this to the young man and he agreed to get married. He wanted the Guru to officiate his wedding. But before it could be solemnized, the Guru passed

away. Saddened at this unexpected event, Nitya Chaitanya
Yati decided not to get married. But the Guru appeared in his
dream and asked him to get married. Though he knew that
it was Guru Nitya Chaitanya Yati who had appeared in his
dream, what he saw was the face of Yesudas. The young man
now felt that he would get married if Yesudas officiated at it.
He spoke to me about it. I did not see it as just something he
had seen in a dream. I took the matter seriously and talked
to my friend Nandagovind. He spoke about it to Yesudas.
'Isn't it a story you have fabricated to bring me to Ooty? Do
you think all this is necessary for that,' Yesudas asked. Still,
Yesudas took the matter seriously and did the needful.

In 2004, when I was the global secretary of the WMC,
we conducted a programme called 'Hridayaragam' in
Chennai, providing free heart surgery for affected children.
Two hundred children who would have otherwise lost their
lives, benefited from this. This was done in collaboration
with the Madras Medical Mission Hospital. N.R. Panicker,
V.C. Praveen and Reji Abraham led the programme to a
wonderful success.

As I look back on my life, there have been many
activities that added value to my life. But the one that stands
apart is what I was able to do in Chennai in 2015. The
incessant rains had brought life to a complete standstill in
the city. Many people lost their houses. These people who
were struggling to make both ends meet had now to bear
the brunt of the fury of nature too. They had to be led to
start a new life. It was not enough to be a spectator; one
had to be the performer. 'Only when your life is useful for
others will it become a blessed life'—these words from the
famous Malayalam poet Asan reverberated in my mind.
I convened a meeting to think about finding a solution to
the problem. I invited representatives of all the Malayalee

organizations and twenty-two organizations across the spectrum of religion, caste and creed attended the meeting with single-minded earnestness.

I was selected as chairman and presented an action plan before the representatives of the various organizations. We decided to build close to a hundred houses for the Tamilian brothers who had lost their houses. Our decision was announced in public. This plan called for a lot of money, manual labour and meticulous planning, and we decided to raise funds for the same. There was an amazing flow of contributions from all quarters. Oommen Chandy, the chief minister of Kerala, contributed Rs 50 lakh. Before making the contribution, he had called us to inquire whether we would accept the help. This call had a rejuvenating effect on our spirit. We expected only a small amount. Instead, we raised half a crore! This was made available from the Chief Minister's Relief Fund.

It was for the first time that the Kerala government had made such a contribution for a relief work in another state. We felt grateful that the state government had understood our sincerity and setting aside all differences of language and political considerations, had given the help. To add to that, the president of the Muslim League, Panakkad Sayed Muhammed Ali Shihab Thangal, came to Chennai with P.K. Kunhalikutty and announced his support to our efforts. This made our enthusiasm multiply many times. They contributed Rs 10 lakh for our project.

Thangal told us that he had been wondering who would organize such a relief measure in Chennai, when he came to know about our efforts. This remark also encouraged the organizers. Innumerable organizations and people who were conscious of their social responsibilities came forward to contribute the material needed for the construction of the houses. Many merchants delivered their products at the work site without taking any profit. We built 110 houses. The success of this project owes much to the immaculate planning and resourceful leadership of M.A. Salim, K.V.V. Mohan, P.N. Ravi, R.K. Sreedharan and K.P.A. Latheef.

Some of the thrilling moments in the film *2018*, based on the floods that lashed Kerala, are very familiar to me as I observed the same in Chennai. If what is shown in the film happened in Kuttanad, what I saw happened in Chennai. As the flood waters rose, people were left with nothing to eat. Lakhs, including women and children, suffered. To overcome this difficulty, we started a community kitchen. As soon as we started bringing the materials for preparing food, the people took over. This proved that even if one person takes the initiative in some useful project, innumerable people can line up to render support. People came forward to cook food, make parcels and distribute them. We had started with the idea of supplying the needy with the minimum requirement of food, but very soon, more than 10,000 parcels were being distributed, without taking any money from others. To add to the enthusiasm of those who were working voluntarily, Kalaipashi, an establishment under Santhosh Murukanandan, came forward to help us in distributing the food packets. With this support, more items could be cooked. The number of volunteers also increased. One can imagine the depth and strength of the voluntary work involved when it is revealed that more than 30,000 packets were distributed every day.

There is a close relationship between the organizations ready to undertake such work and the voluntary work offered by the general public. It is spread to different levels and depths. Once a work is over, another task can come up. Though basically most organizations work for the upkeep and progress of culture, they are willing to take up novel ideas and work for their fruition. I feel gratified that I have been able to be a part of many such projects. It is not possible to limit such work over a period of more than half a century to a few pages in a book. It is my earnest attempt to show the wide variety of projects with which I became involved.

At the time of writing this book, I was the president of the Tamil Nadu chapter of the Malayalam Mission. This is a programme directly controlled by the government for fulfilling a unique aim. The director of the mission now is Murugan Kattakada, a famous poet and teacher. The mission is committed to make the new generation of Malayalees, residing outside the state, to stay connected to their Malayalam roots and language. This work is going on well all over the world. Based on the mission's syllabus, Malayalam classes are held. Book discussions, literary debates and book releases are also conducted to supplement the classes. Whenever I attend any of these programmes, I feel as if I have reached home.

My wife and our children were born and brought up in Tamil Nadu. Generally staying outside the state for a long time will affect the attachment to the state and the language. But in our case, this has not happened. My wife Priya has passed the examination titled Kanikonna, which is conducted by the Malayalam Mission. She is preparing for the next one. Now it is essential to have a knowledge of Malayalam of the level of the Class 10 for those outside the state to be eligible for a job in government departments. Those who pass the examination conducted by the Malayalam Mission can get employment in Kerala. This has led to more people showing an interest in learning Malayalam. Laudable work in encouraging art and literature has been rendered by Kumbalangad Unnikrishnan, a poet and the secretary of the mission, as well as Smitha, the convener. Recently, when the Tamil Nadu chapter of the mission celebrated its tenth anniversary, a documentary titled

Neelakurinji Poothu was screened. I am extremely grateful to director Suja Susan for the help she rendered in making that a great success. Lockdown restrictions due to the spread of Covid-19 gave me the necessary time I could use towards the successful completion of the film.

Modern means of communication has made the world smaller. It is not a small achievement that a person sitting in Chennai can deliver service to any place in the world. This has enabled me to be active in many organizations, both near and far. One such organization is the Delhi-based Distress Management Collective. Advocate Deepa Joseph is the chairperson and I am the patron of the organization. The other patrons are Ananda Bose (IAS Retd), presently the Hon. Governor of West Bengal, Fabian, IFS Retd, Justice Rajan and T.P. Sreenivasan, IFS Retd.

I hold a great degree of respect for the Sree Narayana Institute of Medical Sciences at Ernakulam, established by the devotees of Sree Narayana Guru under the leadership of Dr Rajappan (Chandrika). The institute offers MBBS and PG courses as well as nursing courses. Sree Narayana Guru's blessings gave me a chance to work as the president of this institute for two years. At present, I am a permanent board member. My position as the patron of the Sree Narayana Samithi in Mumbai where 11,000 students are enrolled, and also as the honorary director of the Jubilee Mission Medical College, Thrissur, are some of my most cherished milestones in the field of loving service.

I would also like to share the latest recognition, one that is most sacred to me. I have been chosen to be on the advisory board of the Sree Narayana Dharma Sangham Trust at Sivagiri. This is a divine trust that I have been grateful to be bestowed with. It is with immense pride that I remember accepting the award for spreading the words of the Guru, on the day of remembrance of Sree Narayana Gurudeva.

11

King Oedipus and the Limp

'Poetry is the essence of drama.'

'All the world's a stage and all the men and women merely players.'

'Life is but a walking shadow; a poor player, that struts and frets his hour upon the stage and then is heard no more.'

Most of us might be familiar with such famous quotes. They point to the antiquity and acceptance enjoyed by the art of drama. A play depicts a few incidents borrowed from real-life experiences and enacted on a specified stage within a stipulated period of time. Actors appear before the audience and play their part with the aid of lighting, background and varied intonations in the dialogue delivery. Drama must have made its appearance with the advent of civilization among men. Each play is the result of a group of people making an intense effort to present a topic in a dramatic manner. The main part in this is played by the actors who have to sharpen their dramatic skills through constant practice. Acting is not an easy or simple matter. I can support this statement with my experience on the stage for more than forty years. I do not try to define plays. Sages in ancient times and critics in the modern age have carried out this seriously. Wherever language, culture and literature have been analysed in this world, plays have always been taken seriously. They are prescribed for study in schools and colleges because of their all-encompassing importance. I will not be boasting when I say that I have been involving myself in the world of drama on the merit of my inborn talent for acting from the time I was a student, and I am continuing that with immense passion even today. I can say with humility that dramatics is as much my cup of tea as business. My first steps on the stage were taken before the friendly audience at Ambalanagar, where we were staying. I have been able to keep the same enthusiasm alive to this day, despite a busy schedule.

It was the Malayalee Club at Chennai that helped me establish myself as an actor. It was only after coming to Chennai that I took acting on the stage as a serious matter. It was my uncle Dr Sidhan who inspired me to pursue acting. I became active onstage in Chennai from 1986 onwards, and in 1989, I started acting with my uncle. He had established himself as an accomplished actor by that time. We appeared together for the first time in the play titled *Dharmakshethre Kurukshethre*, which was directed by Satish Babu. My experiences on the stage are innumerable. Let me narrate a few very important ones.

Natakam, drama in Malayalam, denotes that which is inside the *naadu*, the place where we live. In the olden days, plays too, like all other forms of art, were enacted for the entertainment of the royal audience. But as time passed, unacceptable things that happened around the country also appeared in the script of the play. An actor had to portray various thoughts and emotions on stage. Soon, one-act plays and street plays too became popular. The separation between amateur and professional actors became prominent. Many a play has been banned even in Kerala as it posed problems for the people in power. During the period of Renaissance in Kerala, many social misdeeds were addressed by dramatists through this medium.

'Chandalabhikshuki', a famous poem in Malayalam by Kumaran Asan, had been staged as a dance drama recently at Chennai under my supervision. (The poem is about the meaningless practice of segregation based on caste.) The events described in it happened almost a century ago, but the social problems depicted in it continue to exist in many parts of our country even today. That is why such a presentation becomes pertinent today. This is mentioned as an example of the permanence of certain themes in plays. Playwrights in future may choose an old story for their presentation but must use it to highlight how it is relevant even in the present day.

I have had many fortunate breakthroughs in the world of dramas. A family engaged in business usually keeps away from a field like drama, which requires active personal presence. But I have been blessed to be otherwise in this matter; my wife and children encourage me fully in this. They participate in these activities by acting on stage with me on some occasions. They also take an interest in checking the script and in the rehearsals, and even supplying home-made food to participants during rehearsals.

Thirty years ago, it was almost impossible to get women to act in dramas. There was a strong feeling that acting on stage was not suitable for those from respectable families. Even a credible play may have to be shelved if there were many women characters in it. But today, applications from women—from college students to housewives—pour in as soon as a play is announced. It is a tremendous change from searching without success even for one actress just three decades ago. Some of the women who have always stood by me in this field include family friends such as Lakshmi Gopakumar, Usha Jayakumar, Shaila Das and Rajitha. Later, my daughters, Lanchana and Pratheeksha, also joined me.

A lot of people ask me if I experience inner conflict while acting. This cannot be answered in one word. Let me explain. When I have to impersonate a character on stage, there are some preparations to be made. This is not an easy process. As the audience is viewing it live, appreciation and reaction are also instantaneous. Every play requires immaculate planning with regard to the expressions shown by the character, the suitability of the costume worn by the actors, the different shades of meaning to be conveyed through the dialogues, the reactions of those who act together and the timing of the entry or exit as well as the delivery of dialogue. This should not be seen as a pain to be borne but as an essential part of the success of a drama. Each presentation on stage is beset with traps that have to be avoided. One of the most common issues is forgetting the lines to be delivered during a conversation. The actor may have forgotten a particular word and may use another appropriate word, but this needs to be avoided at times. This is because the other person on the stage may not recognize the new word and may get confused.

I must mention what happened on stage at a presentation for the Malayalee Club years ago, demonstrating the need for careful planning at every stage for the success of a presentation.

I was acting as an ardent lover who has come to see his beloved when her mother has gone to the temple. The beloved is alone at home, and it's just the two of us together! I kiss her on the hand. The music that heightens the feeling of love rises to a crescendo. The scene ends with her mother coming back from the temple and seeing us together in that pose. But the person acting as the mother was delayed in entering the stage. The delay was caused because the actress had neglected to note the costume to be worn at that time during rehearsals. The time taken to change the costume caused the delay. The actors on the stage, the person who acted as the beloved and I, were on tenterhooks. Such incidents happen because of the lapses during rehearsals.

Even after many years, *Oedipus* by Sophocles is enacted onstage today. For reference, I acted as Oedipus in that play written and directed by Ajith Kallan. This play was staged in Chennai as a part of the celebration of Dr Sidhan completing fifty years as an actor. Oedipus is the tragic hero fated to marry his own mother without being aware of it. The man's mental agony had to be sufficiently portrayed. Oedipus gorges his eyes out in contrition. I portrayed the role to the best of my ability and was able to win the applause of the audience. But it took some time for Oedipus to leave my mind.

There were many scenes where I got a chance to show my acting skills in this play. At that time, there was a major wound on my big toe and I had to bear the pain while acting. In the front row, major stars, including Thilakan, who adorns the throne of the complete actor in Malayalam cinema, Vishnunarayanan Namboothiri, the famous Malayalam poet, and the famous film actress Jayabharathi as well as many other eminent personalities were present. As the play ended, they came to meet the actors and showered me with praise. My heart was filled with joy. Words of appreciation from such eminent people must be taken as certificates of honour. At that time, I mentioned the wound on my toe and how it impeded my acting. On hearing this, Namboothiri explained how it had to be seen as a blessing. In the Greek story, written 2500 years ago, Oedipus, as an infant was ordered to be killed. His feet were pierced with an iron rod and tied together when he was taken to be killed. The mark of that could be seen on his legs throughout his life. The revelation that the injury on my toe was actually a blessing in disguise for being identified with the character came as a surprise for me. Maybe the term 'blessed actor' refers to such occurrences.

I know today that there are people who look forward to watching me act onstage. This ability was not achieved in a day. There are many names that come to my mind as preceptors who led me to this position. Sahadevan Master, Dr Balakrishnan and N.S. Das are the most important among them. There are those who taught me the rules to be followed onstage and those who corrected me for better performance. Some prominent stars on the silver screen also used to come to watch my plays. Their presence in the audience speaks for the power and influence of the drama. These include K.P. Ummer, Joshy, Roshan Andrews, Hariharan, Sharada, T.R. Omana and many others. I have also acted in many plays with T.R. Omana.

The famous cine actress Urvashi Sharada inaugurated the play *Kaattuthee*. She made a touching speech on that occasion. She watched the whole play and congratulated me for my role as the hero in it. Later, she expressed her desire to act with me. We still maintain a warm equation.

Eminent director Hariharan has also expressed a similar wish. These artists have plentiful expertise and hold the view that an actor has to be familiar with the stage in order to perfect the skill of acting.

The support and encouragement given by Dr Rajendra Babu must be specially mentioned. Dr Babu was the head of the department of Malayalam at Madras University and the son of C.G. Gopinath, a well-known figure in the world of drama. He also wrote the screenplay for the films *Spatikam* (1995) and *Guru* (1997). I must mention S.S. Pillai, who was the secretary of the cultural society named Dakshina. The appreciation for my dramatic efforts from the members of Team Arts stands apart from everything else. Latheef, Soman Kaithakkad, Dr K.J. Ajayakumar and Vallathol Unnikrishnan have always provided me with support and encouragement.

I place a lot of importance to discipline. I insist that everyone is present on time at rehearsal camps and other gatherings. Each rehearsal camp works like a workshop in dramatics. All relevant matters—from the play's intellectual impact to the level of appreciation to be expected from the most ordinary viewer—are at these camps.

Every aspect of the scene has to be meticulously analysed. Otherwise, blunders will reign the stage. If an actor portraying a historical character appears onstage wearing Paragon slippers and sporting Ray-Ban sunglasses, the audience will boo you out. It may be that the actor went behind the curtain and had forgotten to remove it before coming back onstage. Just imagine King Dasharatha and Hanuman with cooling glasses! Or an electronic watch on the wrist of Lord Sree Rama!

No play can be staged in a hurry. The actor must absorb every nuance of the character through constant practise. When I act, there's an exchange of the self between me, Anoop and the character. It may be likened to the transmigration of the soul.

Let me take the example of the play *Kaattuthee*. I acted as Velappan, a blacksmith, a man who had become hardened and unyielding like iron in body and mind by his constant contact with fire and the metal in his workshop. His back was bent by his posture during his work when he had to squat and bend down to blow into the fire. No small measure of practise would be sufficient to impersonate such a character. It was also difficult to remove myself from the character after the performance. T.R. Omana acted as my wife and Sabitha Anand as my daughter.

Though I have become active in films, I'm still more inclined to drama and theatre. I feel proud to be described as a producer who could not visit the shooting sites as he was busy at the rehearsal camp for a play. The experience that I have gained from forty years onstage is priceless. I still associate myself with at least one play a year.

The company of the five-star associates in the business world and that of the artists in the world of drama may not always merge well. But I enjoy both: an enthusiasm that leads to accomplishments.

Even after all these years, I still feel a sort of tension when I go onstage for a new play, akin to the pangs before the birth of a new life. I am sure there will be many in this field who experience it. If anyone claims not to feel it, beware!

12

How I Define . . .

Here are a few words and expressions that we use in everyday conversations. I feel that they have meanings beyond the apparent ones. I feel it pertinent to give my own definitions of a few such words.

1. Sincerity: It is the sum total of responsibility, indebtedness and affection. When all these elements meet, life becomes meaningful. It is also present in doing your duty even at the cost of great discomfort.
2. Life: Life can be defined as a journey from birth to death. It is a responsibility placed upon us by nature. We are not responsible for our birth. But we should complete the journey of life with sincerity and make it fruitful.
3. Love: It is a priceless possession deposited within us. It does not have any external gloss and true love truly touches the soul. One should be able to distinguish between love and affection. All living things have this phenomenon. You see a crow cry in distress when its companion suffers.
4. Honesty: Honesty is a responsibility sprouting from the sincerity that one exhibits to one's own

self. It goes beyond returning what you got from the wayside to the rightful owner.

5. The Past: Each of us is a link in a chain. Without yesterday, there is no today. This reminds us that we cannot be thinking only about ourselves. We cannot create the past. It has its own cause and effect cycle.

6. Silence: Silence is a state of existence. The moment of silence that comes just as the curtain rises for the drama to begin, brings thousands of thoughts into one's mind. It cannot be categorized as anxiety or fear. As one lies with eyes closed in Shavaasana, the Corpse Pose in Yoga, one becomes aware of silence. The silence at dawn has its own music and sound.

7. Difficulty (being upset): The responsibility of overcoming this lies with the one who suffers it. The only remedy is to think deeply and act accordingly. Wrong thoughts will only lead to more difficulty. With practise, one can reduce it.

8. A Day: It is a chance given for us to do something different from what we did yesterday. One has to utilize it by contributing something meaningful to society and the family.

9. Adventure: An action that suits the occasion. When others hesitate, we go for it. It is taking up a difficult responsibility. It is the difficulty in doing something that makes it an adventure. Some adventurous decisions will become important turning points in life.

10. Books: Reading is an inspiration, an enthralling experience. It is revolutionary enough to change ourselves. Books will help us find ourselves. *My Story* by the ruler of Dubai who successfully built

an amazing nation in the desert and *I Am Malala* by Malala Yousafzai are two books that have captivated my attention in recent times. Everyone must find some time to read. But selecting good books is also difficult.

11. Leader: A leader is one who utilizes the abilities of many to fulfill our dreams and shares the result with all. They must consider the opinion of others as they move towards the goal. Humility is an essential quality for a leader.

12. Guru: A guru is one who has knowledge and experience in whichever field they work in. It must be an elderly person, rich in wisdom, with no hint of selfishness.

13. Service: Undertaking responsible actions is service. Some services are compulsory. Soldiers and doctors can be taken as examples. In essence, it is fulfilling your responsibility to society. What you gain from it is self-satisfaction.

14. Hatred: Hatred is an emotion. One should not allow it to remain permanently in the mind. When we place good thoughts in that place, hatred will vanish.

15. Humility: Never think that I am superior to everybody. However high you may rise in life, never allow humility to desert you.

16. Sleep: There is no specific time limit for this. Sound sleep should prepare you for getting the energy for further efforts. You may lose sleep over happy things as well as unhappy things. I have made a film within fifty-one hours and gained a place in the Guinness Book of Records for that. Luckily, I was able to do it without losing sleep.

17. Happiness: A feeling you get when you see something good and experience something good. This experience differs for different people. Recognition from others, the success of what you have produced, the success of an idea you put forth and many such result in happiness. One must strive to find happiness in all that one does.

18. Victory: A situation where you are able to get good sleep with complete peace of mind can be described as a victory. This comes as a part of physical and mental health.

19. Married life: Marriage is a contract between a man and a woman based on equality. Both need to value family relationship. Married life is about coexisting with someone you can equate with mentally. Caste or religion should have no importance in this relationship. Instead, one's ideas must be unbiased and free of prejudice.

20. Neighbour: One must always have care about one's neighbours. Having good neighbours is a good fortune. I had the experience of being forced to shift my office because of my neighbours. All must remember that co-operation is essential among people. No one can live in isolation.

13

A.C. Govindan and Infinite Knowledge

This chapter is about my grandfather. He cannot be restricted to an introduction as simply being my father's father. I came to know the details of his life only at a later stage. But what I have learned needs to be shared.

He was born on 25 February 1896 in the Kothaparambil Arayamparambu family at Kodungaloor in Thrissur district of Kerala. His father was Chathunni and mother Kurumba. He started his life as a clerk and after holding many official posts, rose to become the magistrate. Arayamparambil family has hosted Sree Narayana Guru on many occasions. A.C. Govindan has stated that he would attribute all his achievements in his life to the fortune he enjoyed in meeting and prostrating himself before Guru at this house. My grandfather was a writer of repute. I would like to introduce some of his works as I believe that even in this modern age, his writings are relevant. Many of the passages can be quoted during motivational speeches.

Success in Life (1949)

A book with the title *Success in Life* appeared at a time when no one thought there was a need for any special lessons for success. It was a compilation of the articles that A.C. Govindan had been writing in newspapers. It was a collection of essays meant to show the path of life to the new generation. Readiness to sacrifice and constant endeavour are the qualities specified for success in life in these essays.

I have chosen to practise many of the instructions given there as if it were by a biological succession. These are qualities that reached me through my father.

- One must make maximum use of all of one's abilities.
- You should never give up the first job you get just because it is a small one.
- Show honesty and precision in work.
- Knowledge is strength.
- Perseverance, continuous hard work and self-confidence are qualities that must always remain with you.
- Time must be spent judiciously.
- You must be liberal, progressive and good at heart.

These are all points taken from his essays that can be considered as good lessons for management students today.

There is one chapter in this book titled 'Possibilities of an Hour'. I was surprised to see the views expressed in it. This chapter emphasizes the fact that as per the average lifespan of Indians, what one Indian gets for work is only eight years in his life. He also warns that if our mind wanders like a ship without anchor, we will be heading towards our own destruction. The great thinker also tells us that even if we have more and more money, it will all be of no use to us if there is no peace of mind.

I have quoted the above lines as I am sure that they are all points that can guide the younger lot to a better life.

Mukhaparichayam (An Introduction to Some Great Lives, 1959)

We have seen many history books spanning different periods. But *Mukhaparichayam* is the first book to introduce the genre of autobiographical books. It was the time when speaking about oneself was looked down upon as self-praise. A.C. Govindan inaugurated this new form of writing. This contains the life of forty-four people who have excelled in different spheres of life. This has been rendered in a way that spreads hope and excitement in the readers.

Kuttikalute Sree Narayanaguru (Sree Narayanaguru for the Children, 1965)

The Man of this Age, Sree Narayanaguru, has been described in this work in such a way that it penetrates deep in the minds of the children who read it. There are nineteen short chapters in it. In one of the chapters titled 'Njaan kanta Sree Narayana Guru' (Sree Narayanaguru I saw), he describes the occasion when he met Sree Narayanaguru. It was 1914. I had just completed SSLC. Guru was resting at the Adwaitha Ashram after the annual meeting of the SNDP Yogam. Guru was advising visitors by writing his suggestions on pieces of paper and handing it over to the visitor through his disciples. As the young, seventeen-year-old Govindan did not have the courage to approach Guru directly, he was found roaming around the place. Guru understood what the boy wanted and said, 'You don't need any advice. You are a student. Study well, learn to live as a good human being . . . that is all that you need to do.' He followed this advice literally for the rest of his life.

I too follow this advice. If I had read *Kuttikalute Sree Narayanaguru* earlier, I would have included A.C.

Govindan as a character in my film *Yugapurushan*. He has constructed each sentence in it in such a way that the life of the man who travelled ahead of his time can be understood and emulated by the children.

Kuttikalute Asan (Asan for Children, 1964)

This is a beautiful history book written for children. The readers can understand the depth of the relationship between Asan and the author who has described how both he and Asan walked through the Kozhikode market. He advises the reader to study the poem 'Parikketta Kutty' (The Wounded Child) to understand the purity of the relationship between a mother and her child.

The child in that poem had climbed a small mango tree and had fallen down from it. The child is afraid that his mother may be angry with him for getting injured. But the mother reaches the child and dispels all such thoughts from the little one's mind by saying thus:

Fear not, that I will beat you for this
Cry not, the pain will soon vanish.
The wound you got in innocent play
Will only adorn you, my child.

After saying so, the mother kisses the child on the spot where he had a bruise to dispel the fear in his mind. In just ten lines, Govindan leads the readers to all the ingredients that Asan included in his poems to bring happiness to the readers' mind.

Sambalsamrudhi (Prosperity, 1931)

This was the first book that informed Malayalees about the science of spending money. It is a modern study on economics. The book begins with this sentence: 'The world-famous

Emperor Napoleon was the son of a daily labourer in France.' One of the chapters deals with the study of body language—a subject that has not yet become popular in Kerala.

The author has also written about the importance of a smiling face and an attractive style of conversation, with examples. He speaks about the peace one gains through faith in the Almighty.

Vichaaraveedhi (The Thinking Process, 1929)

This book has the rare distinction of being lauded by Ulloor S. Parameswara Iyer, one of the most eminent poets in Malayalam, as one essential for the development of our younger generation. In the preface to the book, Moorkothu Kumaran, a famous writer, cultural leader and teacher of Kerala, recommended that all the children read this. How to behave with your father and mother? How does one acquire moral values? The importance of reading and making speeches. These are some of the topics described in the book. I feel immensely delighted to have my grandfather crowned as the 'Grandfather of the World'.

I wanted to publish these books once again and was able to do it when Sumesh of Interset Publica came forward to do it. The function to launch the book was held at Kozhikode. That function was blessed with the presence of the descendants of the three most important poets of Malalyalam. P. Arun Kumar, grandson of Mahakavi Kumaran Asan, Uloor M. Parameshwara Iyer, grandson of Uloor S. Parameshwara Iyer and Vallathol K. Ravindranath, grandson of Vallathol Narayana Menon were present on the occasion. The famous novelist and short story writer T. Padmanabhan released the book by presenting it to Minister Govindan.

14

Nayanar: A Politician
with a Difference

Many of the incidents that have happened in my life and
the people behind them still remain fresh in my memory.
Both the great and the ordinary among those people have
added something to my life or have been responsible for
making it better. Some leave sour memories while others
enlighten and inspire. The life lessons that they have taught
me are my precious wealth. There are those whom I care
for and those for whom I care not. My dislikes are my
own. However, I have no interest in creating enemies. If
I find it difficult to get along with someone, I move away.
The propriety that is expected of me when meeting others
makes me humble. But I will not allow it to make me weak
in any manner. Every aspect of my life, from the freedom
that I take with my speech to the philosophy adopted for
my ideas, all have been created with these thoughts in mind.

Former chief minister of Kerala E.K. Nayanar was dear
to me and he allowed me the freedom to tell him whatever
I felt. When he came to Chennai, the Malayalees would be in
a festive mood. Whenever I went to Thiruvananthapuram,
I would get an appointment to see him. There was no trace
of hatred in his being. He used to hold a very popular TV

programme called *Ask the Chief Minister*. Once he asked me, 'Do you watch my programme on TV?'

I answered, 'Yes, I watch it with my family. After we started watching this programme, we have stopped watching the comedy programme *Comicola*.' His laughter upon hearing my reply still echoes in my ears.

On another occasion I got two copies of *Kaalathinte Kannadi* (Mirror of the Times), a book containing his speeches.

It was given to me by Muraleedharan Nair, private secretary to the chief minister. I gave one copy to my friend Nandagovind. Later when Nayanar came to Chennai, Nandagovind wanted to get the author's signature on his copy of the book. So we both went to the place where E.K. Nayanar was staying. We held out the book and requested him to sign it. He took the book and opened it. Looking at us he asked, 'Where did you get this book? Did you steal it?'

Later, we understood the chief minister's reason for the question. The book had not been officially released. Muraleedharan Nair had given it to me because of our close association. The incongruity of our approaching the author himself with a book that had not come out yet had prompted the query from the chief minister.

He then signed the books for us.

His conversations were often liberally dotted with witticism.

Once when he arrived at the Chennai airport, I was among those who had gathered to welcome him. He called me to come near him and asked, 'You don't come to Kerala nowadays. Why?'

'There is power cut in Kerala. That is why I do not come there,' I replied.

'Who told you there is power cut in Kerala? Hey! Mularaleedharan Nair, do we have power cut in Kerala now?'

As Muraleedharan Nair remained silent, he turned to the IAS officers who had come with him and repeated the question. As the uneasy silence prolonged, he said to me in a low voice, 'Shouldn't we have some power before we can cut it?' Then he burst into his roaring laughter.

His words, full of humour, delivered with a smile on his face, were enough to warm any strong opposition.

His wife, Sarada Teacher, checks in with me even today.

15

Some Lessons for Success
in Business

Whether I am with friends or at meetings in universities or even generally, one question that invariably comes before me is about the secret formula for success in business. I try to provide some form of a satisfactory answer, but I still feel it is not enough. Typically, I share what I have understood from reading books and from personal experience. I advise them to imbibe the lessons in them while conducting their business.

I believe it is time for a new work culture to emerge in our country. We will lag behind if we hesitate to give up the traditional methods and accept the modern modes. We should channelize our thoughts in order to achieve greater heights. What we seek must be a favourable change. Success should consume one like an excitement. The old generation should hand over the baton to the new with confidence.

I follow my own method in everything that I do. If you try to follow some method that has brought success for someone else, it may not do so for you. Everything works at its own time and pace. We should understand the strategy that will convert an opportunity into success for us.

I find peace in my work. I do not support any business that destroys one's peace of mind and robs you of peaceful sleep. One must form one's own method. You should allow your business to grow only up to a level where you can control it. Importance should be given to faultless progress. If you fall for enticing temptations and deviate from the right path, you will face difficulties. Money is precious, but it is when it merges with human values, that money attains glory. What you need for success in life is needed for success in business also. I am stating all this basis the warm support and acceptance I have received from the public in the past fifty years.

Doing business becomes a headache for the one who wishes to do everything himself. It will become easy if you find capable people and delegate duties to them. I follow that method. There are thousands of people working in different departments in my company. I entrust them with work with the confidence that they are better than me in their own field of work. I have given every worker in my company the freedom to approach me. Our relationship is one that comes from the heart. The strength of the AVA family is based on that relationship.

My company is built on the strong foundation of confidence, respect and co-operation. Everyone from the first worker to the newest recruit are a part of this group. We all stand together for common welfare and prosperity. There is no leniency in matters of discipline in the work and achievement of our goal, but it is not imposed on anyone. When each one carries out their responsibility well, victory is ensured.

Financial discipline is essential for any establishment—big or small. We have before us examples of establishments that nosedived into ruin by investing the money earned from a known business into something unknown. All company owners must keep in mind the rule of maintaining accurate accounts of income and expenditure, not spending more than what one has earned and of keeping some money in reserve for unexpected events.

Your path in a business enterprise will be smoother if you have the courage to adopt new vistas and the confidence that success is imminent. But there is nothing to replace hard work. Success is something that you have to be patient for. You have to be prepared to face setbacks. You have to ensure that your product and service are of a high quality. Only those who think about the bigger picture can achieve greatness. All efforts must lead towards perfection. For this, one's ability must be improved constantly. It is only on a rough sea that you know the strength of your ship. A crisis or a difficulty is something that can be turned to your advantage.

One must always be aware of the value of time. The reputation of your institution is paramount and one must make efforts to uphold it. You must combine traditional methods and the present-day professionalism in your work. Listen to good advisers. Be ready to learn from your consumers. You must be ready to learn and acquire new technology.

Your plans must not be entirely dependent on banks or other financial institutions. You should depend more on your own money. You can approach banks for further development of your enterprise. If the actions of the management are transparent, you will get more support from employees and dealers. A businessman must have the mind of an ascetic. *Shradha*, devotion, is what leads one to the goal. An individual's growth is the growth of the society too. All expenses that stop the circulation of money must be avoided. Business is just a synonym for trust in the integrity of the other. One engaged in business must travel, read, study and observe things deeply. Your study must help you teach new methods to the market.

All these are general principles. You should never try to imitate the methods of one who has gained victory. Money will make relationships bigger as well as smaller. To suit the times means offering your contributions to society at different times.

- Relationships are important for the growth of business.
- Growth must be bilateral or mutual.
- All transactions must be transparent. Preconceived notions and misunderstanding must be avoided.

The success of a business is not limited to the annual income and profit. A successful businessman is one who can sleep seven hours a day with complete peace of mind.

In 2007, when Dr Sidhan was ill, it was decided that I would manage the South Indian markets, while Pradeep Cholayil, my brother-in-law, would handle the others. It was on this decision that AVA Group was formed. Pradeep, who heads Cholayil Group, manages the rest of India and the foreign markets as well as handling the sole responsibility of the Cuticura brand.

Dr Sidhan's farsighted approach saw that such an arrangement would give us both the freedom to work in our own area of special interest and be beneficial to both companies.

There is some important information that the younger generation of business-minded people must be aware of. I am revealing one of them to warn newcomers to not be trapped in such pitfalls.

An international company once approached us with an offer to buy or rather 'swallow' Medimix Company. It was the chairman who approached me. They were ready to settle for any amount. But we shook ourselves out of the lure of money and said, 'This company is the life of many people. We cannot give up our association with Medimix. Money-making is not our ultimate aim.'

To overcome this answer, they asked me, 'How many children do you have?'

'Two girls,' I replied.

'Once they complete their education, wouldn't you get them married?'

'Yes.'

'But won't your relationship with them still continue?'

'Yes, of course.'

'Think of such business transactions in the same way', is what they wanted to tell me.

Their attempt was unsuccessful. To add to that, we got the foreign brand Cuticura . . . one of the oldest brands in the world.*

There were occasions when multinational companies made concentrated efforts to stall our sales. Their strategies included removing our advertisement boards, threatening shopkeepers who displayed our advertisement with withdrawal of their products from these shops and many more. We were able to rise above all these petty tactics

---

* Cuticura was established by Potter Drug and Chemical Company in 1865. Subsequently, it was acquired by Purex Corporation before being purchased by Jeffrey Martin. In 1987, Dep Corporation took ownership of the brand; later on Muller and Phipps acquired the Indian rights. In March 2001, we acquired from Muller and Phipps.

because of the genuine quality of our products and by using counter tactics.

When our main rival in the market brought their product in their vehicle, shopkeepers used to gather around and take away the product because there was such a high demand for that product. We did not try to make an unhealthy rivalry to that. Instead, we started delivering our product directly to the shops in the rural areas and, thereby, increase our sales. That worked out very well. We would go to the shop and request the shop owner to buy two or three cakes of soap. They bought more only if these soaps were sold. We have never given our products on credit, either then or now. We depended on the psychological attitude of the shopkeeper who had to pay for the two or three cakes. He would try to sell them first so that he could get his money back.

Interestingly enough, we used to visit the shops on cycles.

Gradually our soap garnered a huge demand in the market. Instead of seeing it as a soap to be used for relief from skin ailments, people saw it as something to be used to protect the skin and keep oneself healthy. We are grateful that it was so warmly welcomed in many markets and our growth also gained speed.

However, it was essential to make more people know about our product. How will the people know the advantages to be gained by using Medimix soap? There was no television to catch the eye of the people through advertising on it.

Then, we found a way to do it.

We printed attractive photos of gods and goddesses on cards to be distributed during the festivals. On the other side, we printed an advertisement of Medimix soap. Since the card had the photo of a god, most people accepted the card and kept it safe in the pocket or a bag. A few might have thrown it away, but most others would take it and keep it safe because of the photo of the divine figure imprinted on it.

This gave a lot of publicity to the soap. We printed the advertisement on the covers in which the *prasadam* (offerings made to the deity distributed among the devotees) was distributed from the temple.

We achieved better results from the hand-held fan that we distributed. During festivals, we sold lakhs of fans with the advertisement of Medimix soap printed on it. Air-conditioners were not so widely used in those days. So this came in handy to keep oneself cool during the hot season when festivals were generally held. During the famous Thrissur Pooram, the mahouts of the caparisoned elephants as well as the men who sat on top of the elephant used our fans. It was not very expensive, but we got the best propaganda through this.

Then televisions became common and private channels grew. The advertisements that we ran for Medimix on channels such as Asianet and SunTV are some of my historic achievements.

Sudhir Kariat, son of the famous film director, Ramu Kariat, directed this ad film for us. Renowned play back singer P. Susheela was the background singer. The lyrics were set to tune by a young Dilip. I spent many hours with Dilip for this project. Dilip later became famous as A.R. Rahman who later won the Oscar for his compositions. This song was the first and the last one that P. Susheela sang for an ad film. She revealed this while participating in the fiftieth anniversary celebrations of Medimix soap. She also said that from that day onwards, she too had been using Medimix soap.

It was the Medimix soap that came to be sold in laminated carton boxes for the first time in India. Till then, all soaps were sold in wrappers. The new packing for our soap brought in more customers. In 984, we sold double the number of soaps as compared to the previous year. We got the carton boxes made by ITC, who were till best paper board manufacturers in India.

When the infamous forest bandit Veerappan's hideout was raided, one of the objects recovered was a Medimix soap. When the pictures of Veerappan and the things found in the place where he was staying in the forest were seen by lots of people on television, it brought an unusual and indirect advertisement for Medimix soap too.

Thus Medimix garnered a lot of national attention and it became the official soap in the Rashtrapati Bhavan as well as the favourite of Veerappan!

Pilgrims who visit Sabarimala, one of the most important pilgrimage centres in the world, will not miss the advertisement for Medimix soap. They have been placed on the forest roads, warmly welcoming them to the temple.

16

Kerala and Tamil Nadu: Woven Together

I am writing this in Tamil Nadu. The name of the state came from the language spoken here: Tamil. In that case, the land of those who speak Malayalam must be named Malayala Nadu. But we call our land Keralam. If we go deep into the root of this name, we will find some connections between the history of Tamil Nadu and Keralam.

Historians are of the opinion that the word 'Malayalam' came from 'Tamil'. They have evidence to prove that.

Malaii + thalam = Malayalam. Malaii refers to the mountains, while *alam* refers to valley. So the word means the valley of the mountains. As is evident, Keralam is the valley of the Sahya mountain ranges.

The history of Keralam has deep roots in Tamil Nadu. In the famous book *Tholkappiyam*, the Chera Empire is said to have had seven divisions. They were Venad, Poozhinad, Karkkanad, Chithanad, Kuttanad, Kadanad and Malayanad. Kuttanad exists with the same name to this day. Venad refers to the area around Kollam. This land that was lying together at one time was made into Keralam. The original dwellers of Keralam used to speak Tamil. It is an established fact that Malayalam came from Tamil.

All languages have two parts, the spoken and the written. In Tamil, it is named *Chenthamil* and *Kodumtamil*. It was from Kodumtamil that Malayalam developed. Researchers point out four reasons for this development.

1. This land was separated from the other parts of Tamil Nadu.
2. It was the language used by the local rulers.
3. It was the language that came out of the rituals of the ancient Malayalees.
4. There are some similarities in grammar and pronunciation.
   (Those who want to go deep into the subject may use the suggestions given above.)

Sri A.R. Rajarajavarma, in the first chapter of *Keralapanineeyam,* his authoritative work on the Malayalam language and grammar, has stated his findings on the development of Malayalam from Tamil. According to him, the mother of Malayalam, *Karimtamil* existed from 1 to 500* of the Malayalam era. After 500 years, this language came to be known as *Malayanma* in its adolescent years and after 300 years, as Malayalam in its younger days. We have to use Malayalam to study the antiquity of Tamil to know the authoritative details of Malayalam.

Even today, Malayalam does not enjoy the extensive usage as Tamil does. Malayalam can only be considered as one of the regional languages. The strength of a language is determined by the books composed in it. There are no Malayalam books that can be considered better than

---

* As per the Malayalam calendar, this year is 1199. The Malayalam calendar has been in place since 825 CE.

Thirukural, Akananooru, Puranaanooru, Manimekala and *Chilpathikaaram* in their antiquity, literary excellence and cadence. Tamil received the status of a classical language on the basis of these. The age of the Malayalam books does not go beyond 600 years, while those in Tamil have a standing of 5000 years. In 2013, Malayalam also has got the status of a classical language.

There are some other factors that can be proudly associated with Malayalam. We have swept away the ancient language used by the people of the lower strata of society. The language of the rulers and that of the lower groups was based on caste system. This transformation of the language can also be seen as the cultural progress of the society. As one who works in the field of plays and films, I take word usage of any language very seriously. Malayalam does not have the attractive tone that Tamil has. The special features of a language play a major part in making any art form more accepted by the people.

When we consider the relationship between Tamil and Malayalam, we have to take the films in both languages also into consideration. The first film production company in Kerala was the Travancore National Pictures, started by J.C. Daniel, a Tamilian. The film *Vigathakumaran,* which he made in 1926, started the history of cinema here. Many Tamil drama troupes used to come to Kerala and tour the place for dramatic performances.

We should not forget Sree Narayanaguru when we consider the use of the Tamil language in Kerala. Guru had a friend who lived in Chala in Thiruvananthapuram. He helped Guru study the Vedas in Tamil. He also studied many important epic compositions in Tamil. This is mentioned in *Anukambaa Dasakam,* which he later composed. Guru has also translated many Tamil works into Malayalam.

Tamil and Malayalam are branches of the Dravidian family of languages. You can find a lot of similarities in the letters, words, grammar and syntax of the two languages. K.M. Prabhakara Variyer, linguist and professor in the Department of Malayalam in Madras University, has written an article on the similarities and differences between the two languages. That research-oriented article titled 'Tamizum Malayalavum', which he wrote, has been included in the souvenir published on the centenary celebrations of the Malayalee Club in 1997.

I am still invited to meetings connected with Tamil literature and arts. I evaluate the plays presented at their drama festivals and record my findings. Plays by Kathadi Ramamurthy, Sreevalsan, Y.G. Mahendran, Delhi Ganesh and S.V. Shekhar are quite famous. Messages conveyed by art go beyond the limitations of languages.

17

Spectacular Sights during Travels

There are some sights in the world that continue to thrill us even after we have seen them many times. Most of these are connected with nature.

One such sight is that of the sunrise and the sunset. Sights with the mountains or the sea as the background are exhilarating and calming at the same timer. Jawaharlal Nehru in his *Discovery of India* has described the beauty of Kashmir. For those who have not seen Kashmir, his book provides a rare 'sight'.

Nature exhibits her beauty in varied ways in different places in the world. We first come to know about them from the travelogues written by those who have visited those places. Europeans came to know about Asia from the writings penned by Marco Polo (1271–95). We learn about the ancient history of Kerala from the books written by foreigners who first visited here. The Greeks and the Romans have written about Kerala up to the sixth century. But no serious studies have been undertaken on the writings made in Greek, Arabic, Persian, Portuguese and Dutch languages. Our authorities should take more care to get this done. A study on the culture and heritage of a society is as important as any on scientific subjects. Many nations assign special significance to heritage studies. We have lost much because of neglecting such studies.

Eminent historian Velayudhan Panikkassery has written about the long search for finding the Arabic manuscript of *Tuhfat Ul Mujahideen,* the first book on history in Kerala, in the foreword written to the translation of this work. (Preface to the translation of this book was published in1963.)

Understanding the history and lifestyle of different places will help us better our life in this modern age. Taking diverse trips will be of great help in this. I consider myself lucky to get the chance to travel, read books and get acquainted with a variety of learned people. Travel is an integral part of the study of history. It has a depth beyond the ordinary enjoyment from material things. An adventurous mind is integral to be a traveller. We have seen very recently how the world appreciated the adventurous voyage undertaken around the world by a Malayalee, Abhilash Tomy. Tomy was challenging the feats of the people of Portugal, one of the most adventurous of nations in ancient times. The history of Asia changed dramatically when Portuguese mariner and explorer Bartolomeu Dias discovered that ships could come to the Indian Ocean by going round the Cape of Good Hope. It was by taking this route that Vasco da Gama reached Kozhikode in 1498. We are also familiar with the history of Columbus who discovered America while trying to reach Asia. This is only a brief reference to some of the great men who played a part in removing misunderstandings about geographical boundaries.

The Clean Kenyan Village

I have many wonderful memories from my travels which are fresh in my mind. Once during a trip to Kenya, I visited the

Maasai Mara National Reserve. The park has been named in honour of the ancestral inhabitants of that area. This reserve forest is open to tourists to see the wild animals in their full glory. We sit in specially constructed vehicles while viewing the wildlife outside. The variety and abundance of wildlife here makes it one of the wonders of the world.

Lion, leopard, elephant, giraffe, deer and many other wild animals can be seen here. This is also one of the bio-protected areas in the world. One can see the astonishing view of the crocodiles feeding on the deer that try to swim across the Talek River to reach the valley of Maasai Mara. Different types of animals try to enter the river together. The crocodiles, lying patiently for this, are able to catch some of their prey. Other lucky ones escape and reach the banks of the river. One lives by preying on the other. This is the cycle and balance of life established by nature.

The tribal villages that we visited there were extremely neat and clean. Each one of them, living in dwellings constructed as per the traditional style of the tribe, were careful to keep the surroundings neat.

In the forest, houses were constructed in a circle, leaving a courtyard in the middle. There was a chief for each tribe. Though they were not formally educated, they spoke English well. I felt their habits in keeping their surroundings clean should be imbibed by all of us.

In the tribal primary school, students have to spend one hour every day cleaning the colony. This is a part of their academic curriculum. When the children do this, the parents also come to help them. This establishes the necessity of cleanliness.

I was also impressed by their co-operation and commitment to each other's welfare. There was also a store where they sold their traditional handicrafts.

Qatar

Another highlight of my travels was when I went to see the 2022 World Cup Football matches in Qatar. I was struck by the planning that was evident there. I had visited the country a decade back. It is a small country, 11,437 sq. km in area. Doha is its capital. Oil was first discovered in Dukhan Field, Qatar, in 1939. Extraction started in 1940. The rise of the people who once used to rear cattle and catch fish for a living, seemed phenomenal.

I could see with my own eyes the development that they had achieved. There were many who scoffed at the idea of Qatar hosting the World Cup. But Qatar had made world class facilities including roads and buildings. Beautiful high-class hotels, metro trains and artificial islands awaited hordes of guests.

The most astonishing sight was seeing the airport. I was worried about the suffocating crowds that may be there. I too was wondering how a small country would hold such a huge event, but all my misgivings were proved wrong once I reached there.

It took me hardly ten minutes to complete the formalities and get out of the airport where hundreds of aircraft were landing and departing at the same time. The ticket for the football match was an instant visa for the visitors. They were issuing a visa named Hayya, which could be used as the official ticket for the game. This ticket could also be used free of charge in trains and buses.

The stadium had a capacity of 70,000 spectators. This naturally made me wonder how long I would have to stand in queue to get in. Taking bathroom breaks could pose a problem.

But all these anxieties were proved wrong once I arrived there. One simply entered the stadium through the gate mentioned in the ticket. There was no rush anywhere. From outside, there was no indication that there were almost 75,000 people inside the stadium. There was one toilet for each stall. Food and drinks were also provided. Everything was very well planned and executed. I thought of the foresight of the ruler when I saw all this. The government's planning and execution made Qatar famous all over the world. This led to the country reaping huge benefits in business and tourism sectors.

Why can't we too do so? Why doesn't the abundance of manpower and expertise in planning we possess make us achieve progress?

Amsterdam

I have previously described an interesting incident while at Amsterdam elsewhere in this book. Let me describe another incident which I witnessed there.

We were travelling by road when another vehicle banged on to ours from behind. We were terrified. We imagined how the driver would come out of that vehicle and shout unpleasant words and how the police would arrive there and take us to the police station. I also thought of the people in other vehicles manhandling us for causing a traffic block. Instead, the drivers came out of their vehicles and shook hands. Then they exchanged the insurance papers of their vehicles. No bad words; no tense moments. Why can't it be so in our country?

Panama Canal

My wife Priya and I had gone to Mexico to participate in a meeting of Malayalees. From there, we went to see the Panama Canal. This man-made canal connecting the Pacific and Atlantic oceans has become a part of the history of the world. This international channel for ships has eased transportation of goods and travels between the two oceans.

This canal is 82 km long and is provided with three main locks. When a ship reaches the entrance to the canal, it is stopped there for some time. Then the ship is brought into a chamber and locked. Water is pumped into the chamber to raise the ship. The ship now moves forward through that water.

At the next stage, the ship is raised again in another chamber. Thus, the ship rises to a height of 25 m as it moves through the canal. Once the ship comes to the point of exit from the canal, the ship is stopped, water is pumped out from the chamber till it is at level with the sea and the front part of the ship is lowered into the sea. There is a special chamber for this very purpose there.

To come to the Atlantic from the Pacific, ships have to travel about 15,000 km if they go around the South American mainland. Hence, a great deal of time and money is saved by using the Panama Canal.

When I saw the Panama Canal, I observed a wonderful similarity of its mechanism with our Medimix manufacturing process. We have used a similar, simple method in it.

The vehicles that bring the raw materials, including coconut oil, are parked on the top of a ramp. The oil is brought to the tanks below using nothing but the gravitational force of the earth. From this chamber, the oil is taken to the chamber for making soap using hand pumps. This idea helped us save a great deal of time and reduced the work load of our employees.

The Panama Canal, built a hundred years ago using only human resources, is still a wonder of the world. This man-made canal has improved the economy and financial status of a country. It is worth noting that no one has come forward with an idea to replace this simple method, which goes beyond modern technology.

18

Accursed Words and Some Unusual Occurrences

Many Ayurvedic conferences have been organized in different parts of the country under the leadership of my uncle, Dr Sidhan. It was to rejuvenate the Ayurvedic system of medicine and to make the people aware of the advantages of this system. These conferences were held in Delhi, Chennai, Hyderabad and Thiruvananthapuram. Ayurvedic physicians, allopathic doctors, and those who practised traditional medicine were invited. These were conducted with a view to encourage research and experiments with the traditional and modern systems working together.

In August 2004, a conference was held at Thiruvananthapuram where we decided to invite the Governor, Sikhandar Bhakth, to inaugurate the function. Dr Sidhan and I went to the Raj Bhavan to request him to come for it. While talking to us, the Governor asked me, 'Why did you bring him? You are young. You should come for such matters. Why did you trouble him?' He was referring to my uncle Dr Sidhan.

When we made our request that he should come to inaugurate the conference, he said, 'Am I not an old man? Can we be sure that I will live till your conference? I would suggest that you approach Chief Minister A.K. Antony for this.' So we left the Raj Bhavan.

We met the chief minister with the help of M.M. Hassan, former minister in the Government of Kerala, and he accepted our invitation to inaugurate the conference. On the day of the conference, as the distinguished delegates were clapping happily, we received a telephone call informing us that Governor Bhakth was in a critical condition. Soon after the inauguration, we were informed of the news of his death.

His words, 'Can you be sure that I will live till your conference . . .' feel as if they had been accursed. That meeting which my uncle and I had with the Governor and what ensued still remain fresh in my memory.

19

Death of Dr Sidhan and the Unspoken Words

On the night of 10 February 2011, Dr Sidhan felt unusually tired and he was taken to the Madras Medical Mission Hospital, where he was admitted in the observation room close to the ICU. The doctors who examined him told us that there was nothing serious and that he would be discharged in the morning. So, I started for the Chennai airport to go to Kozhikode for a meeting the next day. On the way, I got a call from Dr Sidhan. 'Come to the hospital now. I have to see you. There is something I want to tell you,' he said in a feeble voice.

I was worried by the sound of his feeble voice and immediately asked the driver to turn back and go to the hospital. On reaching the hospital, I went straight to his room without waiting for any permission from the authorities. He motioned with his head for me to approach him. Though he looked very tired, he was sitting up in his bed, leaning on to the support. His face lit up on seeing me.

As he was about to say something, the on-duty doctor came in. She asked me to leave the room for her to examine the patient. I tried to explain the urgency of my visit but to no avail. Before I could know what my uncle wanted to tell me, I was made to go out of the room.

Very soon I saw doctors rushing along the veranda towards the ICU. I knew it was something serious. The doctor came and confirmed that the condition of the patient was critical. I was shocked. A few minutes later, the doctor came out again and said, 'Sorry, we couldn't save him.'

My uncle had called his wife and son Pradeep at the same time when he called me and asked them to come to him. Before they could reach, he was gone.

The thought of what he might have wanted to tell me hurts me to this day.

His absence was strongly felt when we celebrated the fiftieth anniversary of Medimix. Dr Sidhan continues to live in my heart and mind. What happened that day at the hospital still haunts me. I wonder if it is right to deliberately keep a person, who is nearing the end of his life, away from his dear ones.

How sad is the state of those waiting outside, denied the chance of offering even a last goodbye to their dear ones.

20

Medimix @ 50

Medimix soap was first prepared by Dr Sidhan and his wife Soubhagyam, in 1969, in the confines of their kitchen. Today, after a span of five decades, it has the highest sales of ayurvedic soaps in the world.

The soap truly shares a munificent and glowing history. It is also the story of determination and responsibility towards society. Its history is that of the awakening of life for thousands of workers and their families. The Medimix family has reached the third generation of owners.

In these last few decades, many new products have been added; products with a variety of colours and fragrances. A variety of glycerin soaps, hair shampoos, hand wash and sanitizers have been introduced in the market; however, the strong confidence our customers have in our products has continually strengthened our efforts.

The fiftieth anniversary of the inception of Medimix was celebrated with programmes lasting a year, in 2019–20.

We have two business groups: Cholayil Group and AVA Group. Both the companies celebrated this landmark together.

We entrusted my brother-in-law, my wife's brother Pradeep, his children, Laasakan and Susmera, and my daughters Laanchana and Pratheeksha to prepare a timeline of Medimix's fifty-year history for the fiftieth annual celebration.

We brought the workers, who have been with us since the beginning, and their families together for the celebrations. This made the younger generation realize the amount of hard work and sacrifices all of us have made to build this institution up. The historical research proved invaluable in making the new leaders, who had taken up the reigns of the company, take inspiration from past leadership and workers. As our factories are located in different places, this process of gathering information is not very easy. Still we successfully fulfilled what we wished to do.

We felicitated the first workers, distributors, the sales outlets, auditors and others who were connected with the company. Help was offered wherever necessary. We were also able to help the relatives of the workers who had passed away.

Our aim was to make a kind gesture rather than make it a grand show. We were able to start social welfare schemes in the villages of various states where our factories are situated.

The concluding ceremony of the celebrations was held at the Chennai Trade Center on 16 February 2020.

This was kind of like a big family get-together. Those who worked in the company before, senior workers at that time, and all those who worked with Dr Sidhan in the beginning, were felicitated at that meeting. This included the family friend who initially helped in designing the first cover for the Medimix soap as well as many friends, including doctors, who helped by prescribing the soap and those who were ready to help with loans whenever necessary.

The message we wanted to convey was that one should never forget the path one has traversed. The new generation is unaware of the history of the trials and tribulations of those who began this journey. We deliberately planned all this to make them aware of it. By doing so, we made sure that we were passing on not only the physical wealth but also a part of the struggles to the new generation.

On completing fifty years, we used the phrases '50 years of foam filled with love' and 'the power of 18' for advertisement. Eighteen here refers to the eighteen plant products used for making the soap—the number is important in other ways also for me. This is a number that follows me accidentally or otherwise. The first house that my father bought and his first car were numbered 18. The total of the digits of my birth year 1962, is also 18. We now live on street no. 18. My wife Priya's birthday falls on 18. These are only a few; there are other items also related to this number in my life. Still while flying, I choose seat no.13.

Most people believe the Ayurvedic foundation of the manufacturing process is integral to the Medimix brand. Our customers also believe in it. The thousands who hold Medimix close to their heart bear testimony to this belief.

In the beginning, the soap's cover was designed in black and red. Black holds a special place in the psyche of Tamil Nadu. Then the wrapper was replaced by the laminated carton box.

More changes were brought about in the design of the carton to uphold international standards. There were views in favour and against this. We listened to opposing opinions with a sense of apprehension. But it is a matter of pride that Medimix could stand with the other soaps in the market.

Dr Sidhan displayed the same expertise he had in the making of the soap, in marketing it as well. In those days, advertising was mainly through print media. Advertising with the photographs of film actresses and conducting film nites helped in making Medimix come to the notice of the public. The Film Nite that Medimix conducted at the Kozhikode Stadium on 7 February 1976 turned out to be a historical event. Skit performed by film stars, dances, mimicry, live stunt shows and many other novel items added to the success of the nite.

Medimix has always tried to launch programmes that can better the life of the people and make the product dearer to the users. One such effort was by being the main sponsor for the programme named Hridayaragam, with Kamal Hassan as the brand ambassador, where free heart operations were administered for affected children from poorer backgrounds.

Medimix still follows the traditional manufacturing process.

Medimix products, today, are available in e-commerce platforms too. Apart from hotels, Ayurveda resorts and hospitals also prefer to use Medimix soaps.

21

In Memory of an Intrusion

'Impatience never commanded success.'
—Edwin H. Chaplin

Let me recall an incident where impatience and lack of knowledge led me to a dangerous situation. You may consider it as a warning.

This incident, which still sends shivers down my spine, happened in 1993. I was actively involved in the organization and artistic programmes of the Malayalee Club in Chennai. A rehearsal camp for a play was going on at the terrace of the club. Suddenly, there was a terrifying explosion and dust covered the whole area. As we looked down, we could see people running here and there on the street. A building nearby had been destroyed. It housed the office of an organization.

I ran to the building to find out what had happened. Deadly silence prevailed. The roof had come down. Though I was not aware of the seriousness of the incident, I immediately rushed out of the building. We suspended the rehearsal and returned home.

My family was watching television at home. I too saw and heard the details of the incident that had happened near the club. It was a terrorist attack. Terrorists had bombed the office building. When I realized that I had walked into such a place, I was almost paralysed with shock.

The building could have been bombed again and/or it could have collapsed. Terrorists could have been hiding inside with weapons.

That incident sent shock waves throughout the nation, as eleven people were killed. I had thoughtlessly entered that place when those bodies were still lying there.

When disasters and natural calamities occur, there are people who are specially trained to act under such circumstances. Life-saving missions require an adventurous nature, courage and experience in how to handle such situations.

Those who come to rescue people caught in floods may have to face the heavy rush of water when the embankment, used to control the flow of water, breaks. A different type of rescue operation may be necessary at a place on fire.

Sheer luck helped me escape that attack and allowed me to write this book today. A small piece of concrete falling from the roof might have made things complicated for me.

There was another occasion when I jumped in without a second thought.

It was a disaster that shook the conscience of the whole world—the earthquake that rocked Bhuj in Gujarat in 2001. It was an example of how natural disasters impact our march towards modernization and construction in cities. More than 10,000 people lost their lives. Even more were wounded. I was sadly affected by the cry of those people. I decided to go there in person to offer help. Chakiyar Rajan, who shared a similar view, came with me.

We made no preparations before setting out. We came to Mumbai and then reached Bhuj by plane. The airport had been partially destroyed. The scenes that met our eyes on getting out of the airport were enough to break our hearts. Several NGO representatives who had reached there for rescue operations directed us to where we needed to go. We saw many buildings, schools, hospitals, all reduced to nothing. In a thatched shed, essential commodities were being sold. I saw cakes of Medimix soap displayed prominently there. I came to know that this had been done under special instructions from the health department and the disaster management units as it was feared that epidemics may break out as an aftermath of the disaster.

As the whole place had been destroyed in the earthquake, we had to search a lot to find a safe place to stay. In the end, we found a hotel that had been partially destroyed in the quake. We were able to get a room that seemed inhabitable to some extent. The wall on one side had a crack on it, but we decided to spend the night there. When an earthquake strikes a place, there are chances of more quakes in the same place. So it was extremely dangerous. With this thought ruling the mind, I looked out of the window at midnight. What met my eyes was an unexpected sight. The owner of the hotel was sleeping on a cot in the open. He had chosen to sleep at a place where his life would not be in danger even if his hotel came down. We had paid for being in a dangerous situation. This taught me a valuable lesson—that one has to plan carefully before setting out on a service mission to disaster affected areas.

22

A Good Turn Turns Sour

I generally respond favourably when people approach me for help. Many people come to me with varied requests very often. One such appeal was granted as I felt sorry for the one who made it, but it led to a painful event.

Now I know that one should know the background and mental state of the person who approaches for help and decide whether he actually deserves the support. Here, I will describe two instances that taught me this valuable lesson.

In the initial stages of our business, we used tricycles to distribute our soaps. A Tamil boy who worked with us for distribution is the hero as well as the anti-hero in this incident. He did not report for work for three days. The irresponsible behaviour really irritated me. In an era before the mobile phone, making inquiries was difficult. While everyone agreed that he should be dismissed and another person should be appointed, he showed up on the fourth day. I lost my cool as I saw him stand before me in my office room. He looked dishevelled, his clothes were dirty, hair uncombed and eyes sunken. He looked almost insane.

'Where were you the last three days?' I asked him.

'I will explain all that later. I need Rs 50 urgently,' he replied.

I was moved by his appearance, his tears and his helpless look. 'After all, he is asking only for Rs 50. Even if he does not come for work tomorrow, I will lose only that much.' I thought as I handed him the money.

He ran out of my room as if to do something important. He had rushed out to buy kerosene oil, pour it over his body to set himself on fire.

He was retaliating strongly against his family. He loved a girl. But his people did not approve of that girl. He killed himself to show his protest against his family.

I was shocked to hear this, but his last words as he lay fully burned astonished me even more.

He said that his family had not supported him by agreeing to his requests. Now he wanted them to fulfill at least his last request.

This was his last wish:

'I took Rs 50 as loan from Anoop Sir to buy the kerosene. If you have any love left for me, pay it back to him.'

Then that boy succumbed to his fate, leaving his family in eternal sorrow.

His parents came to me to fulfill their son's last wish. When they held out Rs 50 with tears flowing down their faces, I had to accept it with a heavy heart to fulfill that boy's last wish.

I cursed the moment I had given him the money and the wrong decision that I had taken.

I had given the money to help him in a difficult situation, but it had the opposite effect. This taught me an important lesson about understanding the context of helping others.

There was another incident even more bizarre than this. A family was involved in an incident that went beyond the limits of reality.

There was a popular programme called *Solvathellam Unmai* on a Tamil television channel. Lakshmy Ramakrishnan hosted the show. Those who came on the show revealed the trials and tribulations they had experienced in their lives. Their experiences would shock the viewers and touch their hearts.

In one episode, the hostess introduced a forty-year-old woman. She had come with her two sons, twenty-one and twenty-three years old, respectively. She spoke about the difficulties the family had to face as both these sons were affected by a strange disease.

The two young men were tall and looked strong and well. But they were both ill. Thy could not sit, stand or lie down. Their limbs were not supple. Their hands and legs had started bending too. At first, only one boy had been affected but a few months later, the other boy too started showing signs of being affected the same way. They were staying in a small hut where there was no space for them to live. Now, to add to all this, her husband had left her and his children to live with another woman. The telecast detailed all the difficulties this woman had to face in looking after the young men and making a living for them. It was thought that if the two boys were given a place to stay and proper treatment, that family could be saved. But so far, no diagnosis had been made about this strange condition.

My mind was touched on hearing this pathetic tale. I felt that I may be able to help them. I called Lakshmy Ramakrishnan, who had directed my first Tamil movie *Aarohanam* (2012), and expressed my willingness to help them. I shared my feeling that if they were admitted in a good care centre and given Ayurvedic treatment, they might get cured. I offered to bear the expenses for the tests and the treatment. The organizers of the programme were pleased to hear of my offer and they wanted to make a public announcement of that through another episode. They wanted to show the offer being made directly to the mother of the two young men. They wanted to shoot the episode in my office and this was done without any delay.

When I spoke to the mother about my offer, she joined her hands in reverence and said, 'I saw God.' I could see on her face the hope that her sons would get well with the treatment and come back to her as healthy young men.

We, all of us in my family, slept that night with the satisfaction that we had done something worthy.

But what we heard the next morning shocked us. The mother had hanged herself to death that night.

She must have lived only to make the future of her sons secure. When that was ensured, she no longer felt the need to live.

I know many people who have no one to help them and many who have been deserted by those who should have stood by them. These distraught mothers are like volcanoes that can burst at any moment. Society has a responsibility to provide support to such people. Authorities must make arrangements to provide psychological and psychiatric support to these people.

On the basis of these experiences, I decided to offer help through established organizations instead of giving it to individuals. I now work in collaboration with an institution named Nest and the Nest International Academy and Research Center (NIARC). This institution offers free treatment to those who have some disabilities from birth and those who suffer from very rare diseases. It is one of the biggest charitable treatment programmes in Asia. Contributions made by kind-hearted people make the work possible.

Let me end this chapter by recounting the sequel to the incident where the mother died by suicide. The mother had ended her life after making sure that her sons would get good treatment and a place to stay. Her husband, who had deserted her and the sons, was so saddened by her death that he too hanged himself to death. I see his act as an atonement for the disgraceful way in which he had treated them.

How true are the lines by Kumaran Asan, which may be translated as: 'God has not given man any means for showing another what is in his innermost mind.'

23

A Jammu Kashmir Raid

Laws are the foundation on which cultured societies flourish. When laws are absent or are not followed, the country can fall into anarchy. The first known set of laws were made by the Babylonian emperor Hammurabi. It was in 1901 that French archaeologists discovered this set of laws carved on stone where 282 rules had been found. Almost all the codes of laws of the present day are based on that.

Making the laws for a modern nation is not an easy job. We all know about the 'Tryst with Destiny', the speech made by Nehru, on the challenges to be faced in building the nation after Independence. In his speech, the prime minister mentioned the unification of all the states and union territories of India while maintaining the essential individuality of each part which was important because of a legal matter I had to face inadvertently.

A police jeep stopped in front of my residence and two policemen came in. That was the beginning of the problem. It seemed that there was a case registered against me. There was no reason for the police to come here. Still why did they come? I could not find an answer for that.

The visitors were a police inspector and his assistant. They had brought the file containing the details of the case against me. The case was about the sale of Medimix in Jammu and Kashmir and it had been charged on me since I was the owner. The Tamil Nadu Police had taken up the case against me for the seller in Jammu and Kashmir failing to pay the sales tax. The DGPs of both the states had directly taken the decision to take action against me.

Meanwhile, I put my signature on some papers that the inspector placed before me. Taking the signed papers from me, the officer asked, 'Do you know what papers you have signed now?'

I hesitated to admit that I did not know. So he told me, 'You have signed on your warrant for arrest and on the charge sheet agreeing that whatever is written on it is true.' I felt as if my body was on fire.

Our company has always paid all taxes without fail. Our dealings are honest and transparent. Then how did this happen? We had to pay Rs 36,000. The authorities had sent notices asking us to pay the amount on many occasions, but they had been returned unaccepted. This had led to the issuance of the arrest warrant and the raid on the premises. In reality, we had not received such a notice. The real culprit was the one who avoided accepting notices from the government.

The police officers who had come for the inspection realized the truth from our explanation and they took a very humanitarian and helpful attitude. Verbally, they allowed us some time to pay the tax. This was the best that they could do.

If the police raid had happened today, many new aspects would have been cooked up to make it more sensational.

The old saying, 'A lie can travel halfway around the world before truth can get its boots on' would have been proved true. The media conducting public trials, adding half-truths as they please, has led to the ruin of many companies.

When we came to know the actual facts that led to all this drama, we were flabbergasted. The distributor for Medimix in Jammu and Kashmir had been regularly paying tax to the government, but it had not been accounted for by the sales tax department. The officer who accepted the money had entered it in some other account. The lapse on the part of an officer in Jammu and Kashmir had resulted in this action against me. We paid the money and avoided the chance of an arrest; but it took many months for the warrant to be withdrawn and the case to be closed.

The police had understood that I was an industrialist and a social worker who respected the laws and did everything as per the diktats of the laws. This was why they had taken a lenient and supportive stand in this case.

24

The Birth of the AVA Group

Each birth calls for its own planning and preparations. This is especially true when it is an institution. I have already described the birth of Medimix and the paths that it has traversed.

Dr Sidhan, my uncle as well and father-in-law, who made the product and established the company, had an unusual power of comprehension and business outlook. He was a doctor who shone in fields of industry, art and social service.

Facing oppositions, trials and even threats to life and still leading the company onto the path of victory, all credit for this goes to Dr Sidhan alone.

It was a critical time when my uncle talked about bestowing all the responsibilities as well as entitlements of the business. In 2005, we had gone to Kumarakom in Kottayam district to enjoy the natural beauty of the backwaters while moving about in a houseboat. After that, we went to Kuttikanam. The surrounding scenery of mountain passes bathed in mist was beautiful. We had thought about buying some land there if my uncle liked it. From there we went to Kottayam where we booked train tickets for our return journey. As I had some work to attend to at Kottayam, I had to return by a later train. Though we tried, my uncle could not get a lower berth in the train. So he got on to the upper berth. It was very cold inside and soon everybody was fast asleep. At three in the morning, my wife Priya woke up on hearing a groaning sound. As she switched on the light, she saw Dr Sidhan trying to convey something through gestures. He could not speak properly. She could just make out the word *'Mole'* . . . he was calling her, his daughter. She thought that her father was play-acting as was his habit. But soon, she realized that there was something wrong. He could not talk and could not get down from the upper berth. One side of his body had been paralysed. Realizing the seriousness of the situation, she called the TTE for help. He recognized him, not just as a passenger, but as a former doctor in the railways and an important public figure. Messages were sent and when the train reached the next station at Perambur in the morning, doctors and an ambulance with life-saving equipment were waiting for him.

He was admitted in the hospital as he had suffered a stroke and partially lost the ability to speak.

Along with medication, the doctors prescribed speech therapy as well as yoga. My uncle had never spared any time for exercise or rest so far. But now the circumstances had forced him to start them anew. His mental poise was exemplary. Even the doctors commented his willpower. One's mental strength plays an important part in getting cured as well as in preventing serious illnesses. Mental strength and physical strength complement each other.

My uncle's condition improved and when he was strong enough to move about in a wheelchair, he used to visit our farmhouse and supervise things in all the matters concerning the plants, domestic animals and birds there.

It was at this time that he took the decision regarding the division of the business interests. He took a well thought out decision to ensure the further growth of the business. He divided the institutions into two groups and he instructed me to take up the responsibility of the establishments in South India. His son Pradeep was entrusted with the business in the other parts of India and abroad. This enabled us to take independent decisions. Now when I look back, I still feel immense gratitude for my uncle who took the right decision with a futuristic plan. That sense of gratitude only keeps getting deeper as each day passes by.

This division helped in the growth of both the groups. Both of us became successful leaders of our own enterprises. The AVA Group has been handling Medimix, Melam Masala and Sanjeevanam since 2007.

25

The Future

Perfection is just an illusion.

> 'The full moon has a blemish on it;
> The world must be made for imperfection.'

These words always reverberate in my mind.

I am grateful to have the fortune of living in two centuries.

I have not just been a witness of the scientific and technological progress achieved by mankind but also intervene in it. This book can only hold a small portion of those memories. There is much that remain as thoughts, waiting to come out as written words.

That book would be the life story of my uncle, Dr Sidhan. I am grateful that I have been able to fulfill his dreams to a certain extent. Medimix is now about to celebrate fifty-five years of glory. I have been with the company for the last forty-one years. My joy is the joy of those who have been with me. My intention is not just to increase the turnover; it is my dream to keep the good name that Medimix has won so far.

There are colleagues who have been working with me for more than a quarter of a century. Their happiness, improving the standard of living for their families, giving good education to their children—all these are matters that bring immense joy to me. Today, we share a very warm equation within the Medimix family that includes all the workers. If we expand all of a sudden, new employees will come in and the warmth of affection among the members of the Medimix family that we enjoy now may be lost. I do not want that to happen.

Now our business is at a point of transition. The new generation has started taking up the reins. This is especially important in new ventures where their intelligence and knowledge is being valued.

We hope that the new leaders will follow the path shown by our elders and lead the institutions to further glories. They have come to realize our company's core philosophy that knowledge and foresight must be utilized for the betterment of the society.

On a side note, I have decided to be more active in acting. I handled a full-length role in the latest Malayalam film *Achanoru Vaazha Vechu* (2023). The film's appreciation encouraged me to move on further in that matter. I would like to utilize my experience and ability more in the cinema field. I believe that all changes are prompted by creative endeavour.

This book is, in essence, an expression of many things that have remained fresh in my mind for long. I see this writing as the natural connection between me and the society in which I live. I would not dramatically state that this is a slice of my life. However, I have tried to recount what happened without much embellishments. I am gratified to have completed this task to my own satisfaction.

Scan QR code to access the
Penguin Random House India website